Conservation Science

Conservation Science

A.S. BISHT

AGAM KALA PRAKASHAN
DELHI

First Published : 2003

ISBN : 81-7320-053-X

Published by :
Dr. Agam Prasad, M.A.Ph.D. Diploma in Museology
for AGAM KALA PRAKASHAN
34, Central Market, AshokVihar,
Delhi - 110052.
Ph : 7212195, 7401485/6
Fax : 91-11-7401485

Type setting by :
SAI GRAPHICS
Delhi - 110052
Ph. 7223581, 7223896

Printed at :
SANTHOSH OFFSET
Delhi - 110035

Printed in India

To
My Parents

PREFACE

This book 'Conservation Science' is basically based on my lectures for a period of 10-12 years to the M.A. (Con.) students with a back up experience of long years in Conservation of Cultural property which is also partly reflected in my research papers in various Journals over the years. This attempt, therefore, would help all future students of the National Museum Institute besides students of Museology, Archaeology & Archival studies and also the Conservation/Curatorial Staff in Museums, Art Galleries, Deptt. of Archaeology, Universities etc. since most of the chapters are devoted to important aspects of Preventive Conservation, collective approach and total care/safety of our cultural heritage while on display, in storage, in transit or standing in an isolated place. This is the age of Management and Cultural Institutions should not remain aloof from this as described in the book. This attempt is *First of the series* which I have in mind.

A concept of Curator - Conservator would emerge from the contents of this attempt since many institutions may not have a person for active conservation needed by many of the artifacts in the collection/ protection. Hence the need for passive conservation which can be provided by the Curator or Custodian to safeguard the artifacts in his/ her charge for which he/she is accountable. Artifacts can remain in the state of preservation in which these are received by him in charge if not better. However, he/she in no case attempt active conservation himself/ herself unless trained for the purpose.

This book is divided into five chapters which deal with Conservation History, Examination and Documentation, Preventive Conservation, Authenticity and Faking of artifacts besides Ethics in Conservation. Conservation of art collection has been one of the basic challenges of our times and hope it would remain so for many many years to come unless managed well. Conservation, active or passive keeps the artifacts alive/presentable and therefore, the institution would remain best managed by a collective approach to responsibilities of all concerned in their own sphere of working. It is this joint endeavour which would ensure total safety of their holdings. One never knows something might be going on behind the scene and may go unnoticed to a point of no return.

Factors of deterioration, linkages with environmental degradation, acquisition, examination and documentation of every little information, monitoring of health of the artifacts, collective approach, training of personnel in an institution, impact of mass tourism especially the unregulated lots, disaster planning, authentication of collection, fingerprinting to face legal issues, illegal trade of ancient artifacts, professional ethics and misuse of artisans and scientific data by Art dealers. Curatorial and Conservation personnel if they follow these simple norms of preventive conservation, 80% of safety could be provided to the collection. Moreover, this would bring the Curative Conservation to minimum needed if preventive measures are followed strictly by all.

As I look back in retrospection I find many Conservation personalities who had their impact on me. To quote a few - I salute Late Dr. B.B Lal, Late Shri T.R.Gairola, Late Prof. William Boustead, Late Prof. Lawrence Majewski, Dr. O.P. Agrawal, Dr. Norbert Baer, Prof. W.T. Chase and many others in the profession who have not only inspired me but also at times of crisis helped me out from delusive situations. I am deeply indebted to all of them for every thing that they have done for me.

Most of the former Directors and D.Gs' especially Late Dr. Grace Morley, Late Shri C. Shivaramamurti, Dr. N.R. Banerjee and late Dr. L.P. Sihare, I am grateful to all of them for their concern for me without which I would not have progressed to the position of the Head of the Conservation Department of the National Museum, New Delhi. Most of illustrations used by me in this book are from my slide collection which were taken while I was the Head of the Conservation Department for which I acknowledge the courtesy of the National Museum, New Delhi.

I am also grateful to the present D.G & V.C. National Museum Institute for his encouragement and cooperation extended to me over the past couple of years and keeping me active in the profession having invited me to teach Art Conservation at NMI. Besides Prof (Dr) I K Bhatnagar, my dear friend also owes my gratitude for his continued support to me. Lastly I thank all my colleagues in the profession spread all over India and abroad who have extended or are still extending their cooperation to me in one form or the other whom I can never forget for their love I received from them.

My friend circle may wonder how is it that I have produced this book now after eleven years of my retirement. Firstly my eleven years of contact with my students as a Teacher and secondly as is usually said that nothing can happen earlier than it is destined. There is a third aspect of it which is the wish of the almighty that has materialized now and I have been an instrument in his divine hands. God is truly Omnipresent, Omniscient and Omnipotent.

I am also thankful to my wife and other family members especially my two grand sons Ashu and Abhi, who would continue my legacy further when they grow, for their cooperation even though I might have ignored their personal expectations from me during the past one year while working on the text of this book, God only knows.

Last but not the least I am very grateful to Dr. Agam Prasad, my personal friend and Publisher but for whom this book may not have been produced in such a short time

August 2002 A.S.B.

List of Illustrations

PLATES

CONTENTS

CHAPTER V

CHAPTER I

Introduction : History of Conservation in India

Independent India accelerated the pace of development of our cultural activities as a National upsurge and made everyone in authority awake to the glorious past of India. The great art exhibition held in U.K. which included artifacts from varied collections of many important institutions and private collections in the country gave birth to the National Museum of India, as it used to be called then, at New Delhi. A large number of these artifacts which returned back from this successful exhibition were kept on permanent loan at the disposal of this newly created institution which was located inside the Rashtrapathi Bhavan and was later shifted to its own building in 1960. Since then it has grown systematically and is today one of the largest institution of its kind in Asia. After independence the Archaeological survey of India was reorganized, its various branches and circles were established and large number of monuments and antiquities came in its protective care. The imperial Records office was declared to become the National Archives of India and its various regional branches came into being, the Imperial Library was renamed as National Library, Calcutta in 1948 and its scope was enlarged.

Later several other institutions of National importance like the Indian Museum, Calcutta, Salarjung Museum, Hyderabad, Victoria Memorial Hall, Calcutta and the Allahabad Museum, Allahabad were set up. National Gallery of Modern Art, New Delhi and its branch in Bombay was also established. The Indira Gandhi National Center for Arts, New Delhi was the latest to be established as an autonomous Institution with the central assistance besides the National Science Centres. Side by side various states also organized a state level Museum, the department of Archaeology and a state Archives. Various academies also came into being. The activities of the already existing museums were further enhanced and a sizeable number of our artifacts came in the protection of these institutions.

These institutions both at the centre and at the states were also charged with the responsibility of conservation of their holdings and are supposed to keep the artifacts in their collection well preserved and in no circumstances the art objects should decay in these institutions after their entry in them. However, it is the responsibility of the authorities to do a time to time appraisal in this regard and take all possible measures to conserve their holdings for future generations to see.In India we are very fond of passing bucks due to want of preventive measures to our climatic conditions. Fact of the matter remains that many museums and allied institutions are found wanting at times due to lack of adequate preventive measures which should have been taken well in time and hence the situations in some museums have become grave. Accountability to public, therefore, is the answer and right of information is the way to deter any such mishap which should have been avoided in the interest of our heritage. We must realise here that artifacts do not get preserved by their mere entry into an institution unless measures for passive and active conservation both are taken by every such institution. It is needless to say that through conservation we can keep the artifacts alive or in good state of preservation and in turn institutions could be managed to exist. Institutions cannot survive without artifacts and hence conservation should get priority over the other functions. This year, being 55th year of our independence, is most opportune time to make appraisal of our achievements and also take stock of what needs to be done yet besides challenges which have to be faced, the strategies that could be planned by us as an independent Nation. Before Independence, there were very few conservation laboratories such as the laboratory of the Archaeological survey of India and of the Govt Museum, Madras.The time span between fifties to eighties has seen substantial growth for cultural heritage conservation in India at the governmental level. National Museum, New Delhi had its laboratory established in 1957. In about 50 years period several museums, archives and departments of archaeology and museums in the states and at the centre had in-house facilities for conservation of holdings in their possession. The Archealogical survey of India had its various Zonal and Regional Units and the National Archives of India also had its units at various places. The National Research Laboratory for Conservation was established at Lucknow in the late seventies and later had its only regional laboratory created at Mysore, but its proposed other centres still remain to see the light of the day. A saturation point, even through nobody talks of it, seems to be the fate accomplee for the time being. At the various laboratories of National level we do see stagnation today and the pace of progress seems to have preferred for a pause atleast temporarily. Interestingly enough, I have seen this development as well as the changing scenario right from 1954 onwards. I had the good fortune to work with most of the pioneers of the conservation profession active in their respective fields of specialization. Most of them are away from the scene now or may still be engaged in conservation but in a different capacity. With the retirement of these first and second generation pioneers of conservation and most undesirable situation is, if posts are lying vacant here and there unnecessarily, conservation in India seems to be at crossroads.

It is, therefore, in the fitness of things that the challenges to conservation in India have to rise to match the efforts in various directions keeping in view the great variety of materials requiring conservation whether it is in the collection of a museum or of the historic and archaeological sites or is the documentary heritage in our archives and libraries since the overall facilities remain inadequate to our National requirements. Moreover, to me the problem looks to be more of management rather than technical since the needs seem to increase geometrically but the resources do not. In India, the nature of material to be preserved is certainly diverse in character and is becoming quantitatively huge day by day.

Conservation of cultural heritage whether in the form of monuments, sites, museums, art galleries or archives has been one of the major tasks of our times especially after independence. The efforts of the Government in this direction at the central or state levels got great impetus but keeping the vastness of our heritage, the facilities at our command have fallen short and continue to be disproportionate to our actual needs as an Independent Nation. A sizeable portion of our cultural assets ancient or not so ancient, therefore, remain unattended even today since it is varied, vast, scattered & unorganized. Our efforts to preserve the heritage continue to look for the right momentum due to constraints of resources and lack of public awareness. With the result the heritage is being ignored before our eyes and the result could be anybody's guess. Conservation still has a low priority in our organizational set up and, therefore, has a low budget in most of our institutions responsible for actual conservation of cultural property. The General public has some interest in artifacts as pieces of ancient past out of curiosity but their interest does not necessarily mean an appreciation of the efforts to preserve them. To public, conservation of cultural heritage is a matter of routine, going on behind the scene, though it is through it that we can sustain our heritage for posterity. We, therefore, are not able to muster the public opinion and media attention to plead for our case. At times it has gone against our efforts due to lack of proper interaction with them.

Time and again there have been reports that Taj is getting deteriorated due to one reason or other which include gaseous pollution from nearby foundries and railway yard, suspended particulates, rusting of iron dowels, structural distress, emissions from the Mathura refinery, sand-stroms from the adjoining Thar desert, replacement of damaged marble slabs, drastic changes in the surroundings, use of surface coating which has yellowed and lately the reported fungus growth on its surface. All these show concern from various quarters creating a false impression that the Archaeological survey of India's efforts are not to their expectations. It is, therefore, for the A.S.I to conduct studies on these lines and elucidate the correct position. I personally feel that changes in the look of Taj, if any have to be accounted for scientifically and the over concerns put at rest. I just wonder if such statements in newspapers are based on colour measurement studies or only on the eye or the photographs which at times could be deceptive. Preservation of the excavated sites, the antiquties recovered from the sites and for that matter my proposal for a Mobile Field Laboratory at the excavation site as a first-aid measure is for the coinsideration of the concerned departments. Photogramatic Studies and remote sensing technolgy could be of help in locating new sites prior to excavation. Interaction with concerned experts would go a long way in this endevour. Living monuments pose specific problems. Many times, efforts to preserve, as is where is, are not liked by monks and pujaries as they prefer complete renovation rather than restoration.

The fate of the artifacts in museums and art galaries is in no way better as many of them do not have in-house facilities to execute active conservation maninly because of their low budget and even if there is staff, they are not able to contribute much for one reason or other which at times could be even lack of confidence in them. This is not conducive to the growth of conservation infrastructure. It is our primary function to preserve collections in these institutions, as a permanent resource that we hold in trust. Most collections are meaningful objects and when they reach museums or galleries are in good condition but time after time such objects are discovered to be faded, dirty, crushed by overcrowding, damaged due to mishandling, unscientific repair, damaged by pests and damp, in-adequate storage, improper display, lack of documentation and conservation on modern lines. Many a times harm which natural forces of decay took centuries to do, could be inflicted instantly by acts of neglect and official apathy. Many museums or art galleries have a tendency to remove damaged objects from public view and dump them in their stores. The authorities would dare to dissent publicly from the view that museums acquire or keep objects which cannot be conserved to an acceptable standard. But this principal is not infact reflected even imperfectly in the actual policies of many museums. They go on acquiring artifacts even if they lack in conservation facilities. Any attempt to divert funds for acquisition to conservation of already acquired objects is not seen in the right perspective by some persons in power for reasons better known to them. It is a commonly held fallacy that once an object enters the collection of an institution it is safe and preserved. Nothing could be farther from the truth as objects can continue to decay in a museum for the reasons stated earlier. There is, therefore, a great need for documentation and examination at intervals of collections and accountaibility to be fixed.

Yet another aspect is the lack of scientific studies for deciding the course of action for a conservation project or acquitions to be made for museums. It is regretable that even after 55 years of sustained conservation efforts and all round development of technology this attitude has not settled in India. In western countries it has been possible to undertake such studies because of the fact that they have to look after fewer artifacts and acquisition rules are strict as compared to us. However, such studies would help in understanding these problems better and would also improve the standard of conservation to bring at par with any scientific studies from abroad.

Smuggling of art object is rampant. The old objects are camouflaged very clervely to look like new crafts and exported. Museums also are being cheated by some art dealers of disrepute as faking of art objects has become a means of earning easy money worldover. We should realise these facts sooner the better because we actually do not know how many fakes are being offered to museums for acquisition. Instances are there when badly damaged painting/manuscripts were heavily retouched. Other art objects also were given antique look though these were made recently to forge them. Lately, there have been reports where some burrocrates have been suspected to have links with foreign auction houses. These should be investigated. Mass public condemnation could deter them from such unlawful acts.

To me there seem to be two main reaons for this situation. Fistly the general public has interest in artifacts as pieces of ancient past and of artistic as well as historic content at times but their interest does not necessarily mean an appreciation of efforts to preserve them. We, should therfore, plan appreciation workshops/courses on conservation of the diverse materials all over the country to attract public attention /appreciation. Public interest in conservation is also inhibited by the profession's apparent ex-post facto character since viewed from outside, conservation seems to lack the excitement of activities that involve discovery or creativity. We Conservators, therefore, should take this issue to the public so that conservation of cultural heritage gets significant, public support and attention. With more and more people investing in acquiring Art works they should be interested in conservation of their possessions ancient and contemporary both. The need therefore, is for an interaction between the Conservators and the people having collections.

Secondly, a large number of arifacts which are not in the possession of any government institution (Central, State and Local bodies) need conservation help. In this context the efforts of INTACH in the last few years and the emergence of some Private Restorers on the scene is a welcome step. However, most of the institutions may divert funds for art acquisition to do conservation and non-governmental organisation may seek financial help from the Central Govt., Dept. of culture to undertake conservation on contract basis. Registered bodies such as IASC, INTACH and their regional Institutes/ Centers all over India can muster public support and with financial grants these efforts could be strengthened. The last but not the least we should encourage voluntary organisations and private restorers to take care of the cultural property which is not being looked after by the Central or State governments. These organisations could also act as a resource bank to help in the actual conservation through their members spread in the whole of the country.

I would like to submit here that the conservation profession owes its gratitude to the National Museum over the years , having done its best always in setting various landmarks for conservation profession may be it is the formation of the I.A.S.C. or the initial planning of the Central Conservation Laboratory For Museums which was later converted in the reorganized form as NLRC project here or the project for Restoration of oil paintings and other works of Art of non Indian origin or it is the National Museum Institute (A deemed to be University) where conservation is being taught at Post Graduate and Ph.D. levels. Our vast cultural wealth varies in its range and contents and, therefore, conservation facilities at our command have to be proportionately strengthened either at the level of the various governmental agencies or public trusts or private trusts, or public at large who possess them so that the future of the past could be safeguarded. There is, therefore, a dire need to establish as many laboratories in the country as possible so that no cultural relic remains unattended to or uncared for and also to strengthen the existing ones because only a person or two cannot do the job any justification.

The authorities, therefore, have to take urgent appropriate measures in this direction. The first step could be the establishment of a few regional laboratories under the NRLC on the pattern of the RCL Mysore so that small labs in their region could look for advice/help to them quickly. Every state which has an archaeology department of its own and/or has a museum of its own has to have a state level laboratory. Every institution should also have in-house facilities for conservation.

The next point which I would like to mention is about the cultural history/heritage which is non-physical in the form of our traditions, social customs, religious inclinations, mythical beliefs, secrets of spiritual and artistic knowledge passed on from father to son or *Guru* to *Shishya* by oral recitation to be documented through modern gadgets and thus conserved for posterity. We should take advantages of the strides made by science and technology lately to devise appropriate techniques and also to preserve our non-physical heritage by documenting it before it is too late. Through these traditions and moral values perhaps we can ragain our lost strength as a Nation.

It is indeed heartening to see students specially trained in Art conservation completing their post graduation or Ph.D in conservation from the National Museum Institute. But it surprises when we very often find our students looking for jobs. I wonder why they do not get jobs. Are the jobs not available ? No -They are there but lying vacant. But why? The recruitment rules need to be revised so as to make the M.A. degree earned by them equivalent to the degree prescribed a long time ago. Who is to be blamed? None, but the system which takes time. Institutions, therefore, have to act fast and get the rules revised as per the present day need. What we need is the help of Administrators, Directors of various Departments and Senior Conservators to utilise this young talent. This problem ofcourse, is more of an administrative nature rather than technical and I am sure, solutions could be found. The degree is surely a job oriented one. Enough talent is, therefore, available in the country as on to-day and we must try to keep them in the country so that they are not drained abroad eventually.

CHAPTER II

Examination and Documentation

Traditional priorities of Museums are three eg.

(i) Collection

(ii) Conservation and

(iii) Exhibition or display.

However, in the recent times museums have essentially an educative role and, therefore, exhibition for education has overriding preference over conservation. As a result, the thrust is on minimising active conservation and resort to preventive conservation. This is achieved by controlling the environment in museums, proper storage including visual storage, scientific exhibition/display on modern lines and collaborative approach to stop/retard the decay of artifacts once these are acquired for a collection. All these aims, therefore, point out towards better Museum Management as per latest guidelines on the subject.

Examination of various factors of decay eg. (i) Physical (ii) Mechanical (iii) Chemical (iv) Biological (v) Technological and (vi) Overall care can lead to monitoring of the health of the artifacts at intervals and documenting these factors for longterm safeguarding the rare and valuable collection for posterity. Total safety of the collections have to be planned and ensured. Any change in an object has to be noted and remedial measures undertaken. The technology of their storage, display and handling to be modified as per latest thinking so that the artifacts once these are taken in a collection should remain atleast in the same condition as these were acquired, if not better than how these were received originally but in no circumstances these should deteriorate further after their entry into a collection. Conservation both active and passive should be on priority basis to achive the aims laid down.

2.1. SCIENCE OF CONSERVATION

There are buildings, paintings, art objects, manuscripts and so on which may be termed as heritage of the past. These documents of the past tell us about the people, their art, their thoughts or their relation with each other. It is also connected with the history, aesthetic appeal, archaeological significance, artistic importance and symbolism, and has an emotional appeal because it touches the innermost of man's creative achievements. The law of sciences remind us that all materials are liable to change their normal form and then deteriorate, consequently disappearing which is hastened due to inadequate maintenance. It can, therefore, be said that all those art objects which had proper care and maintenance could survive and the neglected lot faced their end. In fact, the process of alteration or decay starts the moment an art object is created and continues thereafter whereever it might be at present or was in the past. It is because of this hard fact that we have lost a substantial number of our cultural relics especially those made of organic material like wood, paper and textiles etc. which is more prone to decay than the objects of inorganic composition.

Very often it is said that such and such art work is preserved in such and such museum or art gallery or is with that private individual. It would only be partially true statement since by their mere presence in a collection they do not get preserved in true sense automatically. Conservation which includes preservation and restoration both is a sum total of all actions which are taken to prevent decay and all acts that would enhance the life of these cultural relics. This includes legislations to protect buildings and declare certain art works as of National importance and prohibit the people from defacing them, changing them or demolishing them. This is followed by the task of Experts, Art Connoisseurs and Curators. Amongst them we require Architect, Engineer, Chemist, Biologist and a Restorer on one hand and on the other an Art Historian, Historian, Museologist, Custodian and Curator of art collections. A conservation laboratory is like a hospital for art objects where many disciplines interact with one another to form a team. Over and above all this, every one connected should clearly understand the aim, scope, concept and ethics of conservation to establish linkages. Unless the basic philosophy behind conservation is clear, the nature and extent of human intervention cannot be decided for sure. A collaborative effort of all concerned and especially of the Administrators incharge of culture, would go a long way to achieve the task of conservation in totality. Anything shorter than this would be a half hearted attempt which may be disastrous. The principal aim of conservation is to preserve the values and messages present in the cultural property and make them intelligible so that these are clearly understood. Conservation attempts towards better future of the past.

To act effectively towards this aim we have to understand the causes of their deterioration due to natural, inherent, physical, mechanical, chemical, biological factors besides human damage caused by man himself either by neglect or by vandalism or by ignorance. At times the decay which natural agencies did in centuries, human negligence and biological or natural calamities can do in a very short time. Today, therefore, is the age of management and conservation of cultural property also needs this, to take advantages of the advances made by science and technology in recent times. It is true that even with the technology available today we cannot stop the decay process totally but its pace can surely be retarded. We must stop, atleast, the avoidable destruction of art works since once damaged these can never be restored to their original glory even with utmost professional skills at our command. A formidable man made enemy of the cultural property today is the environmental pollution which can certainly be avoided by proper planning of the industrial development needed to improve the economical levels of our people. However, through conservation we must try to save the art works which link us to the past and are a joy for ever.

To provide longevity to art works, therefore, various steps for conservation such as survey and documentation, listing and periodic examination for recording condition of art objects has to be done with all sincerity so that urgent measures for preventive and curative conservation could be started well in time. To prevent deterioration control of environmental factors such as temperature, relative humidity, light/illumination and pollution control has to be ensured besides preservation from display or storage angles or safety of art works can be planned during their transport from one place to another to avoid damage or making adequate arrangement for climatic variations between cities or between countries. These preservation methods have to be adopted whether the art works are in a public institution or are in private possession. Curative conservation/ restoration has to be entrusted to adequately trained professionals rather than to half baked experts. There is a great need for understanding the materials of art objects, their behavior towards decaying agencies and control methods besides skill needed for retrieval of art works very near to their original state in which the artist visualized them at the time of their creation. Truly the art is reborn.

For this purpose a code of conduct for Restorers/Conservators which stands on moral and ethical values is needed, whether it concerns an institutions or a private individual on one hand and the Restorers/Conservators working with the institution or individuals on the other.

There must be a full documentation, descriptive, photographic and graphic to describe the condition of the object, before, during and after treatment. All methods and materials used for restoration must be recorded in detail. This would guide the Restorers/Conservators of future generations.

2.2 FACTORS OF DECAY

Factors of deterioration can be natural and man-made. These can further be described as

(a) Physical

(b) Mechanical

(c) Chemical

(d) Biological

(e) Inherent

(f) Management related

The factors stated above have to be studied by

(i) Visual based on eye

(ii) Examination at magnification under a hand lens (two dimensional) or under a microscope-stereomicroscope (3 dimensional)

(iii) Examination under visible radiation namely ordinary light, reflected light, transmitted light and raking light

(iv) Examination under invisible radiations such as ultra violet, infra red and x-rays

(a) soft

(b) hard and

(v) Autoradiography (neutron activation), if available.

We must look for the following in specific objects.

(a) Metals-nature of corrosion

(i) Present/absent
(ii) Colour
(iii) Thickness
(iv) Extent
(v) Composition
(vi) Superficial or deep seated
(vii) Past restoration, if any.

(b) Stone

(i) Surface incrustations
(ii) Strength
(iii) Salts
(iv) Cracks
(v) Stains
(vi) Damage
(vii) Breaks
(viii) Exfoliation
(ix) Past repairs

(c) Clay

(i) Surface deposits
(ii) Strength
(iii) Cracks
(iv) Salts
(v) Damage
(vi) Flaking in chips
(vii) Past intervention

(d) Paper

(i) Strength
(ii) Acidity
(iii) Physical damage
(iv) Stains
(v) Foxing
(vi) Colour Change
(vii) Fading of inks
(viii) Insect damage
(ix) Binding condition
(x) Old repairs.

(e) Textiles

(i) Physical Condition
(ii) Mechanical Strength
(iii) Insects
(iv) Acidity
(v) Strength
(vi) Stains
(vii) Fading of dyes
(viii) Condition of ornamentation e.g.. Zari etc.
(ix) Old repairs

(f) Wooden

(i) Distortion in plain

(ii) Splits

(iii) Cracks

(iv) Strength

(v) Biological growth or damage

(vi) Condition of paint or gesso or varnish, if any

(v) Old restoration

(g) Paintings

(i) Condition of the support

(ii) Biological decay

(iii) Colours whether sound or loose or flaking

(iv) Whether kept in mounts

(v) Cracks in pigment layer

(vi) Holes and losses

(vii) Tears in support

(viii) Blisters

(ix) Cuppings

(x) Scratches

(xi) Cleavage

(xii) Varnish darkened or not

(xiii) Blooming

(xiv) Past restoration

(h) Miscellaneous

(i) Strength

(ii) Insects

(iii) Salts

(iv) Loss

(v) Condition of other parts like hairs, decorations and other-past repairs.

2.3 ENVIRONMENT AND CULTURAL PROPERTY

Objects of cultural-historical interest are exposed to various kinds of dangers from the very moment of their manufacture no matter whether they are still fulfilling their original function out door or are within the protective walls of a museum. In order to understand the mechanism of decay of art objects we must understand their chemical composition, method of making, alternation behaviour and the interaction of the various agencies of deterioration process which includes the climate as one of the effective parameters which includes humidity, temperature, wind, rain and air pollution besides light. Scientific studies have shown that climatic conditions especially of the temperature and humidity have a profound effect on art objects since both of them accelerate chemical reactions.

(A) Humidity

Of the factors related to climate, humidity whether in liquid state or as vapour is particularly a severe cause of damage to works of art. The alteration of high and low humidity leads to a constant expanding (swelling) and contracting (shrinking) of art objects which are hygroscopic in nature.

High humidity causes iron to rust and bronze disease becomes active in its presence. The corrosion of copper and lead and tarnishing of silver occurs in high humid conditions. In fact most chemical reactions start in presence of humidity such as salts trapped within the matrix of stone and clay objects suffer due to dissolution and recrystallization within their structures giving rise to efflorescence and at times exfoliation because of increase in volume. Humidity is the basis for the growth of microorganisms, which not only infest organic marterials such as paper, leather, textiiles and wood but also attacks stone, glass and even bronze.

Low humidity on the other hand affects paintings, paper, palmleaf, textiles, leather etc. due to loss of moisture content or dessication making them brittle, fragile and breakable with slight mishandling since it affects their flexibility. In India, the southern parts of the country and the regions on the east and west coasts are hot and humid. Most of the regions in the north have seasonal climate which varies over the year. Some parts of Central and Western India remain hot and dry with practically no rainfall. It, therefore, is governed by the altitude, latitude, surroundings, proximity to the sea and to the mountains.

It is, therefore, necessary to record levels of humidity in the museums etc. of the various parts of the country for devising effective control measures. As a matter of fact we have to study the general climate of a place, climate inside a building and the micro climate in the storage cases or show cases in a museum. Thermohygrographs are available for 24 hours or 7 days recording of relative humidity and temperature. These may be acquired by institutions for effective control measures. For example 25% R.H. indicate dry conditions and 75% R.H. indicate humid conditions.

(B) Temperature

Both low and high temperature are indirectly destructive. High temperature would lower the humidity level and in low temperature continuous freezing of the moisture in hygroscopic objects and followed by melting of the frozen water would produce contraints due to changes of volume within the structure resulting into brusting and scaling of surfaces. The action of frost on standing monuments in those regions, which are on mountains would be damaging. The R.H. and temperature of a closed space are interrelated. R.H. of an enclosed space increases if there is a drop in temperature and it decreases if the temperature rises.

(C) Wind and Rain

The eroding effect brought about by salt laden winds in the coastal areas or sand storms in deserts damage the buildings and structures in these regions.

(D) Air Pollution

Damage to our cultural property due to air pollution has played an important role since the 19th century. Industrial emissions, smoke from coal heating, exhaust gases from motor vehicles react with rain and humidity to form acidic compounds that cause lasting damage to stone and metal especially in the open air. Damage is also caused due to it to objects of paper, textiles and leather indoors.

In conclusion it can be said that climate has a lasting and continuous damaging effect on cultural property and, therefore, we have to devise ways and means to retard, the rate of damage by adopting proper climate management technology within the buildings or even outside for standing monuments. For example vegetation, trees, fountains or ponds, the thickness of its walls and materials used for construction all have a bearing on a monument/building both outside and inside.

(E) Climate Control

The norms of control of R.H. and temperature will depend upon the nature, strength and composition of the object displayed indoors. It has been recommended that R.H. may be kept at 55% ± 5 and temperature between 20°C to 22°C ± 2°C. It is necessary to control both these factors.

(F) Air Conditioning

Most important to remember is that these limits should be maintained all the 24 hrs. of the day, every day throughout the year. Anything short of this e.g. an Air Conditioning working only from 9 A.M. to 5 P.M. would do more harm than good. The best means of climate control is air conditioning. In humid climates a higher figure of 55% + 5% may be chosen whereas for dry climates we may go to 55% - 5%. By keeping the windows out we may eliminate winds and by using filteration systems we could check air pollutants. The air conditioning has to be continuous and, therefore, provision for stand-by-generators should be made. It is of course expensive. Adequate funds may be set aside for this purpose atleast by major institutions in the country since it would ultimately be an investment and not an expenditure. Local air conditioning of the particular galleries or showcases may also be planned to reduce costs. National Museum, New Delhi has been using air conditioning very successfully whether it is central air conditioning or local air conditioning. This is being monitored through Thermohydrographs in the various areas whereever A.C. is functioning.

(G) Alternate Technology

Alternately we may devise humidifier for dry seasons and dehumidifier for wet seasons. Humidifiers enclosed in the bottom part of the show case which is not visible from outside could be devised. Silica gel placed inside sealed cases can normalize the relative humidity. It absorbs extra moisture from wet air. For a cubic meter space 500 gms. of silica gel is needed. We need thoughtful display or storage where materials like wood, cotton cloth alongwith paper, textiles and leather could be put together.

On the other hand humidity in small rooms can be increased by keeping plants in pots or humidifiers or khas on windows which could be kept wet every now and them. These days portable dehumidifiers are used to decrease humidity such as supplied by M/S Defensor a Swiss firm.

The latest in this field is Art-Sorb which is being manufactured by M/S Fuji-Davison Chemicals Ltd, Japan and can absorb humidity in wet season and give humidity in dry season 5-1 kg/1m^3. Research has shown that biaxially oriented vinylon film (Bov film) has excellent gas tight and moisture-proof characteristics in order to seal art objects in a planned R.H. by using it.

Besides these curative measures preventive steps such as designing the museum building in such a way that inside of the building can adopt itself by using materials of low thermal capacity or using sun breakers from the adverse effect of the outside season. One such example is the building of the Govt. Museum in Thiruvananthapuram where large use of wood has been made being a place near the sea and also the ventilation system adopts itself as per needs of the season. Shading of windows, walls or other openings could be done. Wooden objects displayed in this museum are in best state of preservation that I have seen during my long active conservation profession.

The need is, therefore, to understand as to what needs to be done when and why besides how it is to be done. Awareness always helps being most versatile preventive measures. Attempts as described above would go a long way for the control of climate inside a building or outside around a building/ monument.

(H) Problems of Excavated Objects

Environment plays a great role in the ultimate survival of art objects and excavated antiquities, whether inorganic or organic in composition. After all the antiquities have remained buried over the centuries in a particular environment which is entirely different than the normal atmospheric conditions. As a law of nature most of the physical, chemical, mechanical and biological decay is bound to get aggravated as soon as these are taken out to face the normal but different atmospheric conditions, since the equilibrium which such objects had attained during their burial is disturbed. Acclimatization with the changed environment resulting into abrupt loss of moisture content of the antiquity accelerates the decay process till such time the object attains equilibrium with the atmospheric relative humidity. Archaeologist, therefore, usually take adequate conservation measures before the actual digging starts because they have been trained for it but they also take the help of a Conservation Scientist to work closely with them. The interaction of their views would ensure, safety of the excavated antiquities not only during excavations but for the post excavation period also. This collaborative approach would help in understanding the mechanism of decay of material objects and the urgent measures likely to be adopted well before the operation excavation starts. This is true about steps of conservation to be undertaken at the site or during their transport to an advanced center of conservation for detailed treatment. In fact the future of the past has to be ensured so that these new findings may be better understood, documented and interpreted for all times to come. This would also help in understanding the history of science besides the history of arts.

Photogrametry, measurement of electric resistance and remote sensing technology which are being used abroad to locate archaeological sites prior to any human intervention are not being used in India. However, we still depend on exploration and surface finds for locating possible archaeological sites. Perhaps there is a need for self appraisal by all concerned who conduct excavations, eagerly get quick information on their findings and then heaps of such antiquities remain dumped, unreported and unpublished what to say of unconserved. This is not a healthy situation and something on priority basis has to be done to ensure their availability for posterity using all our resources, knowledge and expertise now available in the country.

Here the three situations described are (a) objects recovered from excavations of tombs, caves etc. (b) objects unearthed form excavations from the soil and (c) objects salvaged from underwater.

(i) Objects surrounded by air

Objects recovered from excavation of tombs and caves have been found in good state of preservation especially from dry arid zones or otherwise since these were in an environment quite near to normal situations and thus have survived long. Old Chinese bronzes which have been recovered from tombs have remained almost unchanged for a very long time and similarly art treasures recovered by Sir Aurel Stien from Central Asia have also survived well in dry climatic conditions of that area.

(ii) Objects unearthed from undergroud soil

Antiquities while burried underground are in contact with mineral matters, organic matter, water and air. Each of them contribute in their decay differently and depends on the inter-relationship between these factors. For instance an acidic and porous soil will be both mechanically and electrochemically agressive to metals, such as copper but organic matters such as leather, textiles, wood etc. will preserve their substance at the expense of the copper. On the other hand in alkaline conditions and in a deficiency of air it will favour organic disintegration adding biological factors and, therefore, objects made of organic matter when excavated from moist soil would decay faster in normal environment.

(iii) Objects salvaged from underwater

The chemical composition and the PH value of the immersion liquid will have a bearing on the condition of an art object. Such objects should be cleared from whatever soluble salts are absorbed in their surface as soon as possible.

To my mind most of the problems come because of inadequate knowledge about materials under long burial and their behavior to the climatic changes after their retrieval from the underground. The excavation team should be in a position to visualize the post excavation dangers so that they are ready to combat with the urgent situations on their merits. The field laboratory with facility for critical cleaning, treatment/stabilization of some materials to restoration of ceramics and glass has to be created at an excavation site. A trained Conservator can also help in the removal of friable objects from their burial environments. This is very important since many objects may be lost in the process otherwise.

(I) Environmental Linkages with cultural heritage

Over the past decade or so there has been great concern regarding the environmental degradation and its potential dangers to our cultural heritage and community, their linkages and inter-relation. Today the polluted environment is playing a threatening role to the community and heritage equally for the very survival of the ecology around mankind even through according to a popular belief, ours is the only safe planet where life exists. Nature has provided us beautiful surroundings in the form of trees, mountains, rivers, flora and fauna, the seasons, refreshing ozone near the seas or protective ozone layer to save life on earth and a balance between oxygen and carbon dioxide of the atmosphere. However, man with his casual attitude, ignorance, greed and mismanagement has not only mistreated these factors but also his fellow creatures, animals etc. Man and his environment were initially created to co-exist peacefully but it seems that man has forgotten to honour the co-existence. The two, as a matter of fact have to exist for mutual benefit as there is a subtle and mysterious interaction between them. It is, therefore, but natural that nature would also mistreat us in consequence. Scientific studies have proved that we are heading for a disaster because of the ecological imbalance that exists all over and is likely to worsen further in case corrective measures are not adopted immediately. There have been world wide concerns at various levels and also considerable awareness towards cleaner environment. Since the problem is global in nature, the solutions also have to be appropriately global in magnitude and approach.

(J) Linkages with Community

Scientists are alarmingly concerned about increasing levels of carbon dioxide, pollutant gases from the combustion of fossil fuels, effluents from industries, refineries, power houses, large number of aeroplanes in the atmosphere or vehicles on the roads and due to the recycling/accidental fire of plastics so commonly used. Over and above one sees around him large scale deforestation, soil erosion, unauthorized mining, quarrying and stone crushers, fly ash, discharges of sewage and/or disposal of industrial wastes into our life sustaining rivers. The problem is further aggravated by our population explosion and to live in slums as people are running to large cities for jobs. Any amount of development, therefore, gets neutralized in this process and slums thus produced without proper sanitation facilities, contribute to health hazards and spread of epidemics resulting into loss of precious life, property and even deformities in children. Indiscreet use of chemicals, insecticides, pesticides and weedicides not only for eradicating unwanted insects from the houses but also for the protection of our agricultural products and crops has further added to our difficulties.

Production of harmful chemicals such as polychlorinated biphenyls are linked with cancer, birth defects, infertility and liver damage according to a recent W.H.O report. Of deepest concern are those chemicals which enter our food system directly or indirectly. This includes food additives used in its processing, contaminated river waters, hazardous chemical gases to breath, pesticides used to protect vegetables, fruits and even cereals we eat. Unfortunately man himself is responsible for all these harmful additions to our one time cleaner environment. With the result, we are confronted with warming up of the earth's atmosphere and the ozone hole thus formed would allow the harmful ultraviolet radiations to pour into our atmosphere besides accelerating the pace of natural disasters such as fire, flood and earthquakes. This would result into ecological and physical changes in the crust of the earth submerging the land areas near the sea side due to rise in the sea levels. On the other hand man made disasters such as the Bhopal Gas leakage and the resultant fall-out for over two decades now, have resulted into grave dangers to life in and around this area. We must, therefore, take such disasters very seriously so that their repetition any where is avoided at all costs. Problems stated above have global implications and experiences gained by some developed countries could suitably help to save and preserve the ecology especially around the underdeveloped or developing regions. But some developed countries are using many of their developing friendly countries as places where they can manufacture chemicals etc. which have been banned in their countries or to use cheaper technology e.g. dumping of wastes, plastics for recycling. They would not like to do it in their own country because of harmful toxic gases which are produced in the process unless costly technology of a chemical reactor is available to take care of the hazardous effluents. However, the economically poor countries are still helping them to get finished products in an atmosphere which may or may not be environmental friendly from ecology point of view, due to their economic greed to earn quick money.

Our ancient scriptures speak of five essential elements for sustaining life namely the earth, fire, water, air and space i.e. the *'PANCH TATWAS'*. Today our food which we grow and eat, air which we inhale and water that we drink are all contaminated. Besides there is a danger to the ozone layer in the space and global warming especially due to increase in the concentration of carbon dioxide and the atomic explosions. Cumulative effect of all these environmental changes would be detrimental to the very survival of the living beings, the community he lives in and the heritage he has inherited from his ancestors. Advancement of science and technology has given us large number of life saving medicines but side by side new diseases are also coming in the lime light due to degradation of environment and erosion of our ancient moral values. We seem to be fighting against nature and, therefore, very little is expected from it unless we once again start caring about them.

Suspended particulate materials, industrial pollution and harmful effluents from the exhaust of large number of vehicles running on petroleum/diesel products especially by two stroke engines is likely to cross the safe limits, even with the present day number of vehicles, whereas the developed countries have controlled the problem of dust and air pollution in large cities to some extent by planting more and more trees, shifting away of polluting industries and providing them electrostatic precipitators or technology of collecting dust in water jets. The hazardous toxic gases have been controlled by switching over to appropriate friendly technology and the vehicle exhausts have been curtailed by using catalytic convertors made of platinum or using low sulphur content fuels or unleaded petrol or CNG or regulating the speed of vehicles for maximum efficiency. But in many developing countries these measures are still considered too costly to be adopted.

Such measures are now, planned for the metropolitan cities like Delhi, Bombay, Calcutta and Chennai since studies have proved that the suspended particulate matter in these cities are above the safe levels prescribed by the W.H.O. and, therefore, further efforts are needed in this direction to come to the level of other metros of the world. Recent directives of the Supreme Court and the action taken to fine owners of vehicles producing excessive pollution are some right actions in this direction. Cleanliness is another parameter which we have to learn from these developed countries. I am, reminded of sign boards in New York on lamp posts stating that a fine of fifty dollars would have to be paid by the owners of dogs and other pets if they are found to use streets as places to ease. In contrast we have to go a long way in India since one can easily see people easing themselves by the road sides especially in the mornings and the recent efforts of the Government in this direction are welcome. To eliminate pesticides and insecticides scientists are thinking of alternate technology which would use natural biocides and other methods of biological control which would be environmental friendly and conducive to ecology.

In India, *Neem* and its various products have been used for protecting materials from decay due to biological agencies but natural insecticides

'Neemix Bioneem and Margosan' have been recently patented abroad. There are many such natural materials which could be made suitable for use in countries like India, provided research is directed in this direction. This should act as an eye opener for our National Laboratories so that hazardous chemical pesticides could be eliminated and replaced by environmental friendly measures. I feel answers for our problems have to be found in the region itself rather than importing the discarded technology from abroad. However, joint research projects could be executed to find out environment friendly natural materials which could be useful for the global use and also solutions to our common problems connected with the environment, community and heritage. The development plans should be so devised that the approach remains environment friendly and the effluents or waste materials released by the industries are treated so that they no longer pollute the agricultural fields, water, air etc. The need of the hour is to spread the message to make the masses understand that environment preservation is the responsibility of every citizen. Regulations in this regard must be followed strictly by all, rising above the selfish interests and timely change in their approach towards sustainable development which is environmental friendly. Any development, therefore, which would be harmful for the community in any way would be a futile exercise because if the community is going to suffer in the process then there would be no use of such development at all as it is the community whom the heritage ultimately belongs.

(K) Interaction with Heritage

Environment heavily loaded with gaseous pollutants, humidity, dust and other suspended particulate matter have a deteriorating effect on our cultural heritage whether it is a monument or other artifacts made of paper, textiles, paintings of all types, leather and other objects of ethnographic value. These air pollutants of the environment when present beyond safe concentrations not only have a bad effect resulting into their disfigurement but at times have eroding and abrasive effect which would slowly decay them beyond repair if remedial measures are not taken well in time. Air pollution containing sulphur and nitrogen-di-oxides, carbon-mono-oxide, carbon-di-oxide reactive hydrocarbons in the gaseous form and other particulate matter such as heavy metals have a deadly potential to damage stone buildings and statues made of stone such as marble and sand stone. These primary pollutants often combine with the atmospheric water vapour or rain to form even more deadly secondary contaminants, such as acids of various types known as 'Acid Rain'. Lately studies conducted by T. Stambolov have shown the eroding effect of ammonia which firstly neutralizes the free acid of the acid rain form and then forms ammonium salts. However, in presence of nitrifying bacteria these salts are converted again into nitric acid.

The Indian Association for the study of Conservation of Cultural Property in India, organized a National Seminar on Conservation of Cultural Property in the year 1978 with special reference to Air Pollution. Prof. T. Shivaji Rao of Andhra University, Hyderabad, pinpointed the potential threat to Taj from Mathura Refinery. Earlier in the year 1974, the Govt. of India appointed an Expert Committee to study the environmental impact of the Mathura Refinery with Dr. S. Vardarajan, who was connected with the Indian Petro Chemicals Ltd. (IPCL), Baroda, as its Chairman. The Expert Committee expressed by majority vote that there is no need to shift the refinery from its present location. However, Prof. J.M. Dave a former Environmental Adviser to the Govt. of India, gave his note of dissent and warned that Taj Mahal will be ruined in 50 years due to air pollution from the refinery. This has created enough awareness on the subject and the Govt. of India, started monitoring levels of the air pollution between Mathura and Agra which have so far been under limits and also took measures like using only low sulphur crude at Mathura and also building a very high chimney to allow the escape of effluents much above the height of Taj down in the wind direction. It also stopped the coal based shunting yard near Taj and advised the owners of the nearby foundries to shift elsewhere. But some of the refineries which were there before 1983 have filed a suit in the Court to stay the government order and specific judgement has been delayed, with the result that the foundries remained where they were earlier. However, recently they have been ordered to switch over to other fuels or go elsewhere from Agra.

Few years back again a seminar was organised by the Indian Oil Corporation in a five star hotel at New Delhi to take stock of the present day situation of air pollution in Agra due to Mathura Refinery. As I was told, the consensus at this seminar was, that the impact of pollution from Mathura Refinery has not crossed the safe limits so far and a ten point programme of precautionary measures had been recommended in this respect. However, according to a recent report in newspapers quoting Dr. S. Vardarajan says that Taj is about to collapse due to rusting of iron dowels in the area bearing the Stress load of Taj. The Archaeological Survey of India maintains that, on the basis of study conducted by them, there is no immediate danger to Taj but is naturally alarmed by such reports. I am not quite sure about the studies on the stress load bearing area that have been conducted before coming to such a drastic conclusion. I only wish that the findings of such committees are not politically biased and do stand on scientific ethics and actual gamma ray study of the iron dowels in order to locate them and also their internal condition at present, as was done by Japanese in case of the Great Buddha of Kamakura. Dr. O.P. Agarwal, Director General, INTACH, Indian Conservation Institute, Lucknow, in a recent article "Conservation of Taj Mahal - the real problem" has reported that "Pollution is only one aspect and one factor of deterioration and it should not be thought that by shifting the factories from Agra area, Taj Mahal would be preserved. It is imperative that all processes of deterioration are tackled in order to save this unique marvel of world heritage. In order to reach to some final conclusions many more studies are required, not only pertaining to the environmental pollution, but also of all other factors which are causing damage to the Taj."

(L) Future Plans

The study of people like me who have seen Taj at different time of the day before joining the National Museum feel that unbiased studies have to be made of various parameters of decaying factors before coming to conclusions and the laboratory of the Director (Science) at Dehra Doon should do it themselves but its *modus operandi* should be discussed thread bear between the people who know about the problem and the scientific community in the respective concerned disciplines prior to the proposed study at the National level. Nevertheless outside help can be extended if A.S.I. needs it. According to a recent report U.S. side of the Indo-US Sub Commission on Art and Culture is interested in providing a helping hand as a collaborative study on Taj.

Levels of polluting agencies have to be kept minimum by all possible measure including the shifting of the foundries, isolating the monument from traffic hazards, greening all around Taj to minimise the effect of the winds laden with sand, fly ash and dust etc. during summer months. Old marble slab may be replaced by better quality marble with due consideration of the vein direction of these slabs while continuing the scientific studies on its state of preservation a regular programme rather than theoretical apprehensions only, as it has been the case in the past. Monuments like Taj are for the community and, therefore, it is the responsibility of the community to ensure its safety. Every one concerned has to rise above the selfish/narrow thinking on the aspects of environment in general and impact of other connected problems on the safety of our great cultural past.

2.4. ACQUISITION, EXAMINATION AND DOCUMENTATION

The preservation of our cultural property is one of the major tasks of our times. It is true that the efforts of the Government to safeguard the heritage can only be compared to touching the tip of the iceberg keeping its magnitude in view whether of moveable or immoveable nature. The facilities at the command, governmental or otherwise, continue to remain disproportionate to the actual needs, as a sizeable portion of the cultural relics of the past remains unattended and uncared for which is mostly in possession of public. The fate of the artifacts in a museum is in no way better, as many museums do not have in-house facilities to execute actual conservation of its holdings. The efforts of the Government to preserve the art and artifacts of a country are not getting the momentum, as it should have, due to lack of public awareness in this direction and in consequence the heritage, which is rightly termed as 'Resource of the Mankind', continues to suffer and is ultimately lost for ever.

What, therefore, needs to be focused is the necessary strengthening of the governmental efforts and of creating public awareness to contribute in safeguarding the human resources created by our ancestors in the past. The future of the past is to be secured for posterity.

The media, therefore, has effectively to work for this not only to inform the public what the governmental agencies are doing in this direction but also to involve the masses and create among them the most wanted awareness to supplement the cause by way of Press, Radio, TV and other methods. The Indian Association for the Study of Conservation of Cultural Property, the only non-governmental body of professionals in India, had declared 1991 a year in which Government efforts were shown to the public for the first time.

Deterioration of all materials, art objects being no exception, is a law of nature but curative and preventive conservation efforts in this direction shall certainly retard the pace of their decay. We must stop, at least, the wilful destruction of art works which has ever-lasting effects and once damaged these can never be restored to their original condition even with utmost professional skills. Many a time harm, which nature/environment took centuries to do, could be inflicted instantly by such acts of vandalism and neglect by the ignorant masses. INTACH, a voluntary organisation has launched a programme of conservation in the whole of India. Besides this, there are few major laboratories contributing effectively to preserve artifacts.

The Department of Culture, Government of India, New Delhi, has launched a prestigious project to restore artifacts of non-Indian origin and has opened three centers to cater to the need of the hour. Some of the laboratories having conservation infrastructure and expertise are providing short term and long term conservation training courses to create a force of conservators in India to take up future challenges more systematically. However, these efforts contribute, a little. Many more voluntary organisations and set-ups are urgently needed besides creation of awareness and love for artefacts.

There are innumerable examples where monuments, exposed to attack, were tampered with and this resulted in the loss of the architectural sculpture, mural paintings and furnishings which were once part of these cultural testimonies of the past. In India poverty in general, coupled with the art thieves and thief-agents, is aggravating the gravity of the menace. Enlightened public alone can check such acts. Lack of proper documentation adds fuel to the fire.

There is a need for a recorded taped voice in each monument regarding do's and don'ts. With the catastrophic disasters like flood, war, fire, earthquake and volcanic eruptions happening every now and then, public awareness to meet such an eventuality could be created and measures be adopted to meet any such disaster-natural or man-made.

A formidable man-made enemy of the cultural property is the environmental pollution which has generated situations threatening the very survival of the heritage. Harmful gases, toxic chemicals, hazardous pesticide, damaging particulate matters from industry, felling of trees, demolishing of old architecturally significant structure/buildings for creating sky-scrapers-all contribute to the devastation of the cultural assets. Strict laws and vigilant public can alone arrest it. The last but not the least is the illicit trade of art objects. Smuggling of art objects is rampant. The old objects are camouflaged very cleverly to look new (Plate 1) and exported or vice versa. Mass public condemnation could deter them from such unethical/unlawful acts in the country.

(A) Protection for Health of Objects

The problem of examination of icons/artifacts in various temples and museum collections attracted the attention of custodians of these treasures in view of some thefts of idols and smuggling of artifacts in the recent past. Many of them are of rare aesthetic beauty and comprise a part of our unique wealth of ancient past. It is no wonder that some of them were smuggled out of the country or may have already been replaced by modern imitations or could be smuggled or replaced even now. Lately legal battles had to be waged and enormous sums were spent in tracing some of them and recovering them back for the country. The problem was felt in the absence of their systematic study, documentation including their comprehensive finger printing based on scientific study and it was very difficult to retrieve them back for want of authentic data on them. It is an unpleasant truth that a vast portion of our heritage housed in our museums, monuments, art galleries and private possessions is still undocumented as per latest thinking on the subject and is, therefore, prone to thefts or smuggling aborad. It would be recalled that millions of rupees have been spent on their acquisition but the money spent on their scientific study, documentation and authentication resulting into their protection remains to be inadequate. This fact unfortunately is not unknown to art dealers of disrepute and smugglers who are on the look out for such loopholes. They could even engage people who know about artifacts, their history, art as well as science/technology and may lure them to earn easy money. It is amazing to hear views of some of them propagating for not undertaking any scientific study on them with a fear of being challenged in a court of law.

Time and again there are newspaper reports to this effect which are very alarming. According to a report in the Hindustan Times dated June 6, 1986 published from Delhi the exquisite Sivapuram Bronze Nataraja idol (valued at over Rs 1.5 Crores) and another idol worth Rs 75,000/- belonging to the Tiruvelkudy Manavaleshwara Temple near Mayiladuthurai in Tamilnadu returned from the U.S. after a long battle. The Pathur Nataraja case at the Royal High Court, London was yet another unique example. As early as 1983 a news report appeared in 'India Abroad" being published from New York by Schehbez H. Safrani, "Asian Antiquities from Sotheby's which showed high prices being offered at their annual auction for Indian Art abroad. This is continuing unabated for the past three or four decades. A full-page account published in the Hindustan Times dated May 28,1989 'Looting of Art herritage' by H.Bhasin Pal shows how our art is being smuggled to Western countries. The Nav Bharat Times, Delhi dated 5 November 1995 also published a detailed report. 'How safe are these Gods and Goddess' by Shri

R. Kumar Singh. Besides artifacts from archaeological monuments, the thieves have not spared even our museums whether of National importance or of state level. You name one and you would find it on the list. The latest is the report "Messing Around with priceless Legacy" by Saikat Neogi, published in Statesman, dated 30 August 1998 which is mainly based on a public interest litigation filed by an advocate, Harihar Pratap Singh, with the Delhi High Court praying for facts. Such news items are very alarming. It is high time when we should find facts in these reports and bring to books the thieves and the middle man who are not bothered much about these thefts because they roam scot-free with the alleged connivance of some people in authority. These are example of only a fraction of what has either gone elsewhere or are later traced. I am sure there are many more such examples and if timely action is not taken by our various departments to document scientifically and protect our ancient artifacts, the time is not very far when we will have to travel abroad to see some of these examples of our ancient artifacts. It is, therefore, necessary to review our policy on the matter and document/fingerprint our artifacts without further lapse of time.

Moreover, as per administrative guidelines and in order to detect any loss of artifacts from a museum collection, there is a provision of physical verification of collection periodically. Many smaller museums often get the collection of one section verified by the collection incharge of another section of the same museum. This is not a satisfactory procedure since I suppose the authorities are serious about the spirit of the subject. Collection of various sections of a museum should be got verified by independent, preferably retired experts from other museums of long standing keeping some alarming reports on the problem in view. This exercise has to be done at regular intervals to detect a loss or replacement as early as possible.

Similarly health of museum artifacts has also to be got monitored by conservation experts from other museums or from those experts of long standing who retired from the same museum. The idea behind such a proposal is not to malign the image of anybody but to ensure safety and health of museum collections in an organized way. Museums should monitor the health of their artifacts at the time of their entry as well as at intervals thereafter regularly. National museum, New Delhi can provide a lead to other museums in this aspect.

Late Dr S. Paramasivam had initiated one such project 'Fingerprinting of Bronzes', as early as 1982 in consultation with the Scientific Adviser to the Ministry of Defence, Govt of India. Later the Dept. of Culture asked the National Research Laboratory for Conservation of Cultural Property, Lucknow to arrange a meeting of the various experts and Museum Directors to discuss this project. However, not worth mentioning happened as a follow up. Earlier Dr.Baldev Raj had reported feasibility of such a project and Dr Chandrasekaran of Forensic Laboratory, Chennai had investigated the use of laser excited micro chemical analysis and macrography for characterising bronze idols. A couple of years back Dr. Baldev Raj, Director Metallurgy and Materials Group, IGCAR, Kalpakam submitted a proposal on fingerprinting of South Indian Panchaloha Bronze idols to the Dept of Science and Technology which he proposed to undertake in collaboration with the Govt Museum, Chennai. The DST provided a grant of over Rupees 92.212 lakhs for the purpose. It is learnt that a three year project was agreed to by the DST and the 1997 Kalpakam contact programme was a follow up of the same project. The scientific community has been eagerly awaiting the achievements of this project so that the scope could be extended to other important collections of the country. The author had started some preliminary work in this regard before his retirement from the National Museum that he would like to share with Conservation Scientists. Some equipment for Macrophotography was imported from Japan under the cultural grant and a proposal for a high kilovoltage x-ray of 350 KV was submitted to the

Japanese Government under the 2nd instalment of this grant. This equipment for hard x-rays has since arrived and has been installed recently. However, such a project of importance is yet to take a shape that could very easily be undertaken now as regards the bronze collection of the National Museum, New Delhi is concerned. A few macrographs of the Phopnar metal images including a hard x-ray of one of these seven metal images (Plate 2) was done at the Escorts Ltd. workshop at Faridabad and who were using such an equipment to see defects in castings at their foundry. The results have been very rewarding and if such a study is undertaken in respect of other metal images particularly of those which are of National importance, it would deter their thefts and smuggling abroad. This of course was not possible then but now it is feasible, as the high kilovoltage x-ray machine is available in house, in the National Museum, New Delhi also. It is hoped that, the National Museum, New Delhi would take steps in this direction to protect its valuable collections.

(B) Proposed Study

A feasibility study of preliminary status was conducted on one of the metallic images from Phophnar in the collection of the National Museum, New Delhi and a miniature painting. This study comprised of macrophotography to record details and radiography using soft (Plate 3) as well as hard x-rays to know the inner construction/defects, if any, especially in case of hollow images cast by the lost wax process. These are some attempts in this direction. A systematic comprehensive project for fingerprinting our artifacts is vital from the cultural heritage and also from art historical point of view.

In this detailed scientific study we can gather data on their external features which are unique and hence would be signatures of each of them being characteristic in respect of an individual artifact. Hence for protection, scientific analysis and documentation of our artifacts the following systematic programme is of utmost importance.

(a) Scientific study, analysis of the various constituents of the artifacts and alteration products/deposits, textual, graphic and photographic documentation (visible and invisible radiation), from all angles, microscopy, cross sectional study of the method of fabrication of the artifacts and comparative study of similar artifacts in other collections has to be undertaken.

(b) As a consequence the data storage and retrieval of information gathered from (a) above so that authentication becomes systematic, meaningful and its retrieval becomes quicker using computer imaging.

(c) Inview of large scale faking, forgery, connected problems of smuggling and replacement, no object should be acquired for a collection without proper scientific study and documentation.

(d) Study of associated materials especially in case of excavated artifacts should be completed before any chemical treatment is undertaken to conserve them. A small portion of the artifact treated to be left untreated to take care of the legal aspects to prove ownership/provenance. Attempts should not be made to remove everything from the art object and to deter the general criticism of over cleaning the artifacts.

(e) Minimum intervention from active conservation point of view and more emphasis is to be laid on passive conservation methodology so that integrity and historicity of the artifact is maintained rather than large scale reconstruction.

(f) Artifacts when sent for exhibition for long periods should be studied and compared with the data available with the museum or owner after their return and if documentation on such object is not available it should be completed first before sending them abroad.

(g) The scientific study should be non-destructive as far as possible since we are dealing with artifacts having artistic and aesthetic importance. The study has also to be specific on various parts of the same object.

(C) New Approach in Documentation

One of the acquisition modes by museums has been through art purchases. There are, therefore, two categories of artifacts i.e. those which are already in the collection of a museum and those which are being acquired every year. The ideal situation in respect of new additions to be made for collection would be to examine them scientifically, document them in toto and also authenticating them before their purchase is finalized as is being done by many major museums abroad. Simultaneously the existing collection need to be examined, documented and authenticated as a regular programme as is being done to physically verify them. This would not only document them but it would also monitor their health at regular intervals so that conservation measures may be taken well in time to deter any mishap which could be avoided keeping the interest of the artifacts.

The various findings textual, graphic and photographic (visible radiation and invisible radiation) could be stored in a computer as a data base using computer imaging whereever needed. This would not only provide information about artifacts but would provide impetus to scholars and scientists alike. These could be easily retrieved if stolen by proving their lawful ownership in any court of law in the country or abroad.

Such a study would also provide to the scholar their history of art but also the history of science about which we know very little so far since a systematic study of collection has not been conducted atleast in India. Major museums and archaeological departments can come forward to achieve such a goal. The National Research laboratory at Lucknow could undertake such a programme in respect of smaller museums which do not have such an in-house facility for which it has been created by the central government. Major museums could also collaborate with other National Institute such as BARC, IGNCAR and P.R. laboratory at Mumbai, Kalpakam and Ahmedabad respectively.

2.5 DOCUMENTATION IN CONSERVATION

(A) Documentation Need

In the past there have been problems in the absence of documentation whether it is in connection with the protection of museum collection or health of artifacts it houses or the treatment which has been undertaken without caring for consequences or has been unscientific or improper display/storage/transport/negligence/ignorance. As per latest thinking on the subject documentation in a Conservation Laboratory is equally important as for a museum collection or archives or archaeological heritage. The proper recording and documentation of both new acquisitions and existing collection in the possession of a cultural organisation can hardly be overemphasized. This includes the photo documentation. It is a pity that documentation of our cultural heritage in most of the museums, archives and on archaeological materials excavated or standing monuments is either far from actual needs or incomplete. Most of the holdings under the charge of these institutions have not been documented as per latest thinking and practice as in advanced countries for financial or other constraints and, therefore, remain prone to pilferages due to neglect. This complicates the situation in the event of a possible theft or replacement in a museum, archives or archaeological collection or standing monument or site involving the loss. It becomes impossible to provide legal accountability to them in the court of law, especially in foreign countries, having been illegally taken out of the country of their origin.

In the recent past a couple of such cases of legal ownership had to be proved and we were caught napping. Mostly it is said that there are a large number of artifacts to be documented scientifically and hence the shortcoming. This is not fair and ethical as it is a primary professional responsibility which no one should escape by an argument of lack of resource. Persons who are at the helm of the affairs have to take up proper steps to document their holdings seriously, sooner the better. Institutions of National importance should have proper record of their holdings besides data about other important collections at one place for quick retrieval of informations on their collections especially the art works of National importance i.e. National Art Treasures. Large museums of the country should, therefore, use modern technology of storing information and its quick retrieval using computers and optical disc technology of documentation. These equipments have provision to update the data on these infuture. As regards conservation is concerned, during the last three-four decades, a considerable development in this direction is seen in India especially in the conservation laboratories of bigger museums where people realised the importance of such a documentation work at the All India Museum Conference held at Mysore (Sept 19-23,1973) which was organized by the Museums Association of India. It would be ideal indeed if each object of a museum could be documented from the conservation angle thus subjecting them to all the necessary examination physical, chemical, biological, graphic and photo documentation of the condition even of the best preserved objects unaffected by any deteriorating agency, would, after a lapse of a few years, show a changed condition, the change may be ever so little, but it would be there. This would be extremely important from the art historical point of view and would give an insight of the problem of decay, howsoever small it might be. But alas! so far it has remained only a dream since the collection are so large and infrastructure at command is so meagre. In the National Museum, New Delhi, the priorities got mixed up and nothing substantial could be achieved as regards this aspect is concerned. We even had plans to fingerprint our art object by using X-ray etc. especially the bronzes and paintings to start with.

(B) Problem

However, the National Museum, New Delhi, could devise and implement a policy of preparing treatment record of all art objects which come to the Laboratory for curative conservation. Ten information sheets (Appendix -1 to 10) were devised material wise which would contain information on a particular object for future reference showing also the details of the intervention done. These are kept in the Laboratory and one treatment record is given to the department concerned. This would help to pinpoint the source of hazard as their decay in future could be monitored. This would provide a host of data which could give an insight into the relationship between material, environment, efficacy of chemicals introduced, its aesthetics and products of decay at a later date. Thus the information gleaned from a record of chemical conservation work could well be a contribution to the history of art as well as to the history of science.

There has been an all round urge for such a data base study worldover. In India, however,many laboratories and Restorers working independently have not cared to think about the shortcomings of not keeping any record of the intervention attempted by them or even if they have some record on them they usually have not passed them over to their successors. This has created an alarming situation and have increased the work of future Restorers/ Conservators since it would be necessary for them to know what intervention has been done by the Restorers of the past before they decide what to do now. This is ethically and aesthetically wrong. If they were conscious enough of such a situation cropping up in times to come or were large hearted to share information with fellow workers the problem would be shortened as it could provide valuable information about decay of art objects and materials introduced in them as part of the preservation and restoration treatment processes undertaken by them on one hand and the environment causing continuance of the decay process. National Museum, New Delhi, however, was in know of this responsibility from its inception. Over the past four decades, therefore, such treatment record sheets/cards and their storage (Methodex-Cardex System) has become time consuming and difficult especially for quick retrieval of any information on the object treated in the past.

(C) Prospects

The conservation Laboratory of the National Museum, New Delhi was successful to get trained Documentation personnel for this purpose so that the records could be reorganised and we felt a dire necessity of a computer data base to come to our rescue for storing the vast information and its quick retrieval for reference and study. This of course is one of the many aspects of documentation actually needed and there are seven more aspects of documentation in totality, which are intimately related to actual conservation as detailed below. Such a comprehensive documentation would not only be essential for documentation of conservation work but also could be used in teaching at the National Museum Institute of Art History, Conservation and Museology.

1. Scientific data on analysis and technical study to record information on provenance, dating and authentication.

2. Data on conservation materials, equipments and their suppliers in India and abroad.

3. Data on bibliography in conservation-architectural and chemical conservation both in relation to moveable and immovable culture property.

4. Data on library holdings including slides and other audio visual including video cassette related to cultural property in general and conservation in particular in important libraries of the country connected with conservation.

5. Data about Conservations/Restorers/Conservation Scientists and areas of their specialization.

6. Liaison with other scientists working in National Laboratories through the Dept. of Science and Technology and storing of data on them and their works.

7. Information on international bodies such as ICCROM, ICOM, IIC, ICOMOS, UNESCO on conservation matters to be recorded as data bank and on important laboratories world over.

APPENDIX I

TREATMENT RECORD OF WOODEN OBJECTS

S.No Examiner :

Date received : Date of Return :

Owner :

Acc. No. :

Brief Description :

Provenance :

Period :

Shape and Size :

Number of boards or pieces :

Species of wood :

Condition :

(a) Strength :

(b) Distortion in plane :

(c) Splits :

(d) Biological growths :

Painted/Unpainted :

Nature of Paint :

Conditions of Painting :

Photographic record :

Negative No. :

(a) Black and White (b) X-ray

(c) Colour (d) Macrophotographs

(e) Slides (f) Others

Scientific Analysis (if any)

Treatment proposed :

APPENDIX 2

TREATMENT RECORD OF PAPER MATERIALS

Date Received :

Owner :

Acc. No. :

Subject :

Author :

Provenance :

Period :

Size :

Painted/Unpainted :

If a volume

(a) Number of pages :

(b) Number of illustrated pages :

(c) Bound /Unbound :

Nature of the paper :

(a) Thickness :

(b) Wt/Sq.m :

(c) Layers used to make it :

(d) Identification of material :

(e) Sizing material :

(f) Others :

Alterations in the paper :

(a) Strength :

(b) Acidity :

(c) Physical damage :

(d) Biological damage :

Examiner :

Date of return :

(e) Stains :
(f) Foxing :
(g) Colour change :
(h) Fading of writing :
(i) Others :

Nature of Binding
(a) Type of Binding :
(b) Wt/sq. meter :
(c) Nature of material :

Alteration in the binding :
(a) Strength :
(b) Condition of covering cloth/paper/leather :
(c) Physical damage :
(d) Biological damage :
(e) Others :

Photographic record
(a) Visible Light :
(b) Ultra-violet Light :
(c) Infra-red light :
(d) X-ray :
(e) Macrophotograph :
(f) Microphotograph :
(g) Slides :

Any other observations :

Treatment proposed

APPENDIX 3

TREATMENT RECORD OF TEXTILES

Date received	:	Examiner	:
Owner	:	Date of return	:
Owner	:		
Acc. No.	:		
Brief Description	:		
Provenance	:		
Period	:		
Material	:		
Size	:		
Painted/Unpainted/Dyed	:		
Colours visible	:		
Ornamentation	:		
Condition	:		
(a) Physical	:		
(b) Insects	:		
(c) Acidity	:		
(d) Does it require another support?	:		
(f) Stains	:		
(g) Fading of dyes	:		
(h) Are the dyes fast to washing	:		
Condition of Ornamentation	:		
Others	:		
Photographic record	:		
(a) Negative Nos	:		
(b) Details of photographs	: Black/White & colours		
(c) Macrophotographs	:		
(d) Microphotographs	:		
(e) Slides	:		
Scientific study (if any)	:		
Treatment Proposed	:		

APPENDIX 4

TREATMENT RECORD OF METAL OBJECTS

S.No. : Examiner :

Date of received : Date of return :

Owner :

Accession Number :

Brief Description :

Provenance :

Period :

Shape and size : (diagram if necessary)

Brief History :

Name of Metal :

Physical Condition :

Nature of the Corrosion :

(a) Present/absent :

(b) Colour :

(c) Thickness :

(d) Extent of core :

(e) Composition :

(f) Extraneous incrustations :

Photographic record :

(a) Negative Nos :

(b) Photomicrograph :

(c) X-ray photographs :

(d) Details of photographs :

Scientific Analysis (If any) :

Treatment propossed :

APPENDIX 5

TREATMENT RECORD OF MISCELLANEOUS OBJECTS
(Other than metal, textiles, wood, paper and paintings)

Date of received	:	Examiner	:
Owner	:	Date of return	:
Acc No.	:		
Brief Description	:		
Period	:		
Provenance	:		
Material of the object	:		
Shape and size			
Condition	:		
(a) Physical	:		
(b) Insects	:		
(c) Salts	:		
(d) Others	:		
Photographic record			
(a) Negative Nos	:		
(b) Details of photographs	:		
(c) X-ray	:		
(d) Marco and Micro photographs	:		
(e) Slides	:		
Any other observations	:		
Scientific Analysis (if any)	:		
Treatment proposed	:		

APPENDIX 6

TREATMENT RECORD OF STONE

S.No.	:	Examiner	:
Date received	:	Date of return	:

Owner	:
Acc. Number	:
Brief Description	:
Shape and Size	:
Material	:
Condition	:
(a) surface encrustations	:
(b) Strength	:
(c) Salts	:
(d) Cracks	:
(e) Stains	:
(f) Damage	:
(g) Breaks	:
Photographic records	:
(a) Negative numbers	: B/W or Colour
(b) Light source	: Visible light/U.V/X-ray
(c) Number of prints with the report	:
(d) Macrophotograph	:
(e) Petrographs, if any	:
Scientific Analysis (If any)	:
Treatment proposed	:

APPENDIX 7

TREATMENT RECORD OF PAINTINGS

S.No.	:	Date of return	:
Date of received	:	Examiner	:
Owner	:		
Acc. No.	:		
Brief Description	:		
Shape and size	:		
Structure	:		
(a) Support	: Paper/card board/fabric/wood		
Technological peculiarities	:		
Technique	:		
Condition	:		
(a) Frame	:		
(b) Stretcher/mount	:		
(c) Support	:		
(d) Ground	:		
(e) Paint layer	:		
(f) Surface film	:		
Other Observations	:		
Photographic record	:		
(a) Negative Nos	: Black and White		
(b) Colour	:		
(c) Slide	:		
(d) X-ray	:		
(e) U.V./I.R	:		
(f) Micro/Macro photographs	:		
Scientific analysis (if any)	:		
Treatment proposed	:		

APPENDIX 8

TREATMENT RECORD OF OIL PAINTING

Date of receipt : Examiner :

Acc.No. : Date of return :

Name of artist :

Tittle :

Date/period :

Type of painting :

Size :

Shape : rectangular/round/oval/square

Physical condition

I. Frame :

II. Auxiliary support :

Stretcher/cradle :

III. Support :

Canvas/Wooden panel/Paper :

(a) Loose :

(b) Dirty :

(c) Tears/cuts :

(d) Holes :

(e) Lined/Reinforced/ Not lined :

(f) Dents :

(g) Previous restoration :

(h) Others :

IV. Ground :

V. Paint layer :
(a) Cracks :
(b) Flaking :
(c) Cupping :
(d) Blisters :
(e) Scratches :
(f) Cleavage :
(g) Losses :
(h) Shrinkage :
(i) Discolouration :
(j) Earlier restoration :
(k) Others :

VI. Surface Coating :
Varnished/Unvarnished :
(a) Cracks :
(b) Scratches :
(c) Disolouration :
(d) Blooming :
(e) Others :

VII. Photographic record :
No. of Negatives :
(a) B/W :
(b) Colour :
(c) X-ray :
(d) Macrophographs :
(e) Microphotogaphs :
(f) Slide :

VIII. Scientific Analysis (if any) :

IX. Proposed Treatment :

APPENDIX 9

CARD INDEX

Accession number of the object : PHOTOGRAPH

S.No of the treatment register :

Object :

Material :

Condition :

Treatment given with date :

Name of the person or persons who attened to the object :

File No :

Photo and size...........as above :

Photo negative No. :

Bibliography :

(Publication if any) :

APPENDIX 10

TREATMENT RECORD

Date : Photograph

Acc No. :

Card Index No. :

Negative No. :

Treatment Given :

CHAPTER III

Preventive Conservation

3.1 PREVENTIVE MEASURES

Under the present situation when the number of museums and the artifacts they house, it has become all the more important to maintain them well so that curative conservation measures are reduced to minimum. Nevertheless artifacts do remain in good health by providing preventive steps to check their further deterioration. To me, in a museum art objects should not suffer any further decay if personnel holding the responsibilities of their long life act professionally well,

One of the main functions of a museum or a gallery of art is to preserve its collection. In fact, the process of alteration or deterioration starts, the moment an object of art is created and continues even when the object is in the museum. All materials are liable to change their normal form and then decay, consequently disappearing though the time of their survival would depend on factors of varied nature.

There are various factors which cause decay of objects and can be generalized as below :

(1) Effect of Environmental conditions (temperature, humidity, pollution and physical strain)

(a) The object has faced in the past and

(b) It has to face after its discovery or entry into a museum

(2) Biological or micro-biological activity especially in case of organic material, its past infection and spreading of it to the other objects of similar nature already in the museum collection

(3) Accidents and neglect at any stage.

(4) Lack of proper facilities for preservation.

It can, therefore, be said that the objects which had proper care and high quality maintenance survive for their ultimate discovery, and consequent entry to an art collection and the others, the neglected lot, face their end. It is because of this hard fact that we do not have many surviving examples of our ancient art, especially the objects made of organic material like wood, paper, textiles etc. When an object is acquired for a museum, it is, infact, the beginning of the story rather than its end. It is for the Custodians of the collections to see how best they can maintain their collection, preserve them for posterity, interpret them and display them for the present and the future generations to see and enjoy collection of particular museum or art gallery.

A question is often raised whether an object should be chemically treated or not. There are mainly two theories which are put forward by art historians in this regard. Some people have a feeling that whatever alteration has occurred in an object is of historic value and should not be disturbed. While others feel that the decay in an object should be looked into and properly treated so that the object may be brought to its original form, or very near to as it was made by the craftsman in the past. Doubts are, therefore, put forward whether to administer any preservative treatment to art objects or leave them as such. This to my mind is the greatest problem before the present day Conservators.

Present day advancement of the various branches of science and their application for the above purpose is available by which this process of alteration and decay can be surely retarded if not stopped altogether. It is for the present day Custodians of art collections to decide and to derive best out of it by providing adequate funds for conservation and facilities, not only in terms of money, but also as a moral booster. Proper functioning of the laboratory in their charge should be kept up for all times to come.

Let us consider that a mural painting has been coated with a shellac varnish in the past for one reason or the other. In this painting the main figure is appearing to have some green cloth on the body. On examination, it is found that the shellac layer on top has yellowed with time and is cracking. Because of this the paint has a cracking tendency alongwith the varnish layer. Now, if we leave it as such, a time would come when the paint would flake off and only a few traces of paint would be left, if not today then after a few years. On the other hand, if the painting is properly examined, the composition of the paint, varnish etc. are found out and a suitable solvent is used to dissolve the varnish and not the paint, this painting can be properly cleaned and fresh tested, transparent varnish can be applied on the painting. This would save the painting from further cracking and flaking of paint also. In this process of cleaning, the green dress referred to earlier would become blue, its original colour, for no fault of the preservation treatment or the Conservator.

This is a problem which has to be understood by all properly. The fact is that the blue and the yellow colours together would look green.

Suppose some copper coins are found in an excavation. These coins have thick corrosion of penetrating type or non-penetrating type. Now if the coins have to be preserved alongwith the alteration products we cannot see the inscription or the details of the coins and at the same time if the penetrating type alteration product is not neutralized, the coins would decay from within and a time would come when it would be reduced to powder only. If the inscription is not allowed to be exposed then for what purpose we have excavated it. On the other hand, if we do properly examine the alteration products, we can suitably devise a method by which the inscription can also be exposed for interpretation and the penetrating type corrosion as well as other corrosions can be neutralized. In this process, the incrustation would be thinned down to a minimum or sometimes removed and the coin may now have the so called new look. Incidently, it can be added that these coins eventually would have the noble patina though at times the patina could be artificially produced also, if desired.

Very often, we have wooden objects which developed cracks in them and it is feared that the cracks are increasing (Plate 4) inspite of the controlled environment. It is now a point to consider whether to allow their decay beyond repair, or to treat them. We can introduce wood preserving material in it but we would not know whether the crack has widened or not unless we fill the crack with fresh wood or wood filling mixture because if there is any change, the new material filled would crack first and the joint would widen. After treatment, on the first look, the object may seem to have an altered look, but on the second look, the additions would show distinctly. It would be understood here that the treatment has been done to provide strength to the object and to minimize the risk of further damage. If the added portions are not retouched, these would certainly look ugly and would attract our attention first. A compromise, therefore, has to be made. A well trained Conservator knows how far to go and where to stop.

Sometimes, we have very important documents on paper (Plate 5) which have been written on both the sides of paper and the paper has no strength. It has cracked and pieces are falling apart. This cannot be saved unless given a support on both the sides with transparent cloth or laminating sheet. If after treatment, the visibility of the writing has lowered slightly or its look has changed, it cannot be helped. The question at the moment is to lose it or let it be seen by future generations also. The answer could be anybody's guess. We do keep in mind that the conservation treatment given is reversible.

At times, broken stone sculptures and tarracotta objects are acquired for the museum. These cannot be displayed or handled for study unless repaired. Proper adhesives are used for joining them, but the actual problem is whether the losses at the joints are to be filled or not. Since filling of the gaps would help in the consolidation of the joint, usually filling is done and the new added material tinted to match with the rest of the object. Though effort is not to match it completely with the surroundings, yet some people feel that in this process the evidence of history that the particular sculpture was broken at any time has been concealled and the object has a new look. I think, there, is no harm in doing so. The cleaning of the surface accretions to a bare minimum so that the under details become visible has to be attempted carefully and if in this process the object has to be cleaned it cannot be avoided since exact details of the sculpture can only be seen then.

Corroded bronze or brass images pose yet another problem and need a skill of high degree to tackle them. In bronzes there are two types of corrosion products. Firstly, non-penetrating type which forms a layer of accumulations to some thickness on the object and hide the details under it and the second is of the penetrating type which eat away the metal (Plate 6) and is generally known a 'bronze disease'. In the first case the corrosion products have to be thinned down so as to expose the details and the original patina or the look of the object is maintained. But in the second case, if the corrosion is wide spread, there is no other way out except to neutralise it completely and remove the incrustations, as far as possible, as a last resort. Intermediate methods if applied would give rise to problems because there are chances of the chloride being trapped inside, which would eventually have a tendency to come on the surface. This, of course, is a ticklish problem and a satisfactory method has to be evolved. If the chloride encrustations are in patches, these can be controlled to some extent by sealing them from the atmosphere or stabilizing them with organic chemicals. But, in case, it is desired to see the details underneath also, a compromise has to be evolved in which the "disease" has to be controlled and at the same time, the hidden details are also exposed.

These are some of the points, based on scientific reasonings, which have to be considered as far as actual conservation is concerned. Many more can be cited. Since the authority lies with the Custodians, it is for them to choose and tell what they expect of the Conservators in the profession. Conservation scientists on the other hand should know that a best Conservator would be the one who knows that his job is of utmost importance, he should have a proper understanding of the problems in this field, he should know the exact nature of the objects he is handling, he should use only the tested materials and processes of preservation, he should know how far to go and where to stop while giving preservation treatment to art objects and he should know that the preservation techniques used by him are required to be reversible. There should be no communication gap between the authorities and the Conservation Scientist who should be able to put up his case and problems before them in the right perspective.

3.2 COLLECTIVE RESPONSIBILITY

The traditional museum priorities are acquisition, conservation and exhibition for education and interpretation of collections. In most recent times the second and third priorities have been interchanged as more and more attention is paid by the society and the political authorities today to the educational role of museum especially of those which have been declared of National importance. There is increasing pressure to minimize conservation and preservation in order to make collections more visible, communicative and accessible to the general public. Even storage are no longer the same as these were a few years back and these are becoming secondary exhibition areas by way of visual storage. Emphasis is now laid on preventive or passive conservation because through it, a greater number of artifacts could be attended to since their number is increasing day by day. It has, therefore, become necessary to re-study the question of environmental and other parameters and their effects upon such objects. On the basis of improved knowledge thus gained we can arrive at more objective guidelines for the care of collections as a whole rather than conservation of a very small number of artifacts by way of active or curative conservation which is elaborate and time consuming.

In this context there must be closer study of such environmental factors, air-borne pollutants, light, vibrations besides day to day handling of museum collections, display, storage, transportation within the various sections of a large museum for various purposes, travelling exhibition, house keeping and protection against man-made disasters like war, fire or natural disasters like floods and earthquakes. In order to fulfil these requirements a collaborative approach of all concerned (direct or indirect) is the need of the hour. Care and protection to me is not only the job of the laboratory but of everyone in a museum from A to Z. Through such a collaborative approach we can certainly avoid decay of museum objects-physical, chemical and biological after their entry into a collection. Many times ignorant human hands can cause more damage to the collection than any other factor. Collections can also be protected from mechanical factors of deterioration by taking certain fundamental precautions.

It is a misnomer to believe that objects get preserved automatically by their entry itself into a collection. Infact the responsibility of the museum starts from this point onwards which can be termed as collective responsibility to stop/retard the process of decay natural or man made through ignorance or negligence. Proper identification of symptoms of decay and correct diagnosis of the problems is the first step to remember by all concerned. Since curative conservation needs special expertise we should lay stress on passive conservation for which scientific academic background is only optional. What is needed is the proper management technology, complete understanding of the decay process and the decay which could be easily avoided before it happens. Such an approach would help immediately.

(A) Curator Conservator

Even through we have over 400 museums now in India, the facilities for curative or active conservation are far from proportionate to our needs. However, we may not have a trained conservation specialist in every institution but we are supposed to have a trained Curator in every museum or art gallery. The emphasis, therefore, should be on training, the Curator for preventive or passive conservation. For this special courses should be organized by museums of National importance. This would ensure total care of the collection in order to save it from decay which could be avoided by taking preventive methods of preservation.

There is, therefore, a strong argument for the creation of a Curator Conservator who will be more involved in the preventive care and protection of collection, in the museum rather than its micro sense. There is thus a great need for interaction between various sectional heads of a museum to chalk out an effective conservation policy under the guidance of the Director. No object should deteriorate further after its entry into a collection. This should be possible at practical levels rather than at theoretical concept only. The concept of total care, therefore, should be the ultimate aim of the museums from conservation point of view. Every Curator has to know what to do and what not to do. Some of these steps are detailed under as a 17 point programme.

(B) Collective Approach for Total Safety

1. Acquisition of only the original objects may be adhered for filling the gaps in a particular museum collection. Fakes and forged objects should be discarded at this level. Awareness of this aspect is important. If a Conservator of long experience is inducted in the Art purchase committee it would help.

2. Registration method should be standardized. Use of methods such as putting a seal with stamp pad ink has to be discarded. Curators and collection incharges should not put their signatures on the body of the object especially at the back of the paintings with soluble ink or ball point pens. Accession numbers should be recorded in water proof ink i.e.. indelible ink and not by anything which is handy. This should also be put at a place of a textile which is not so important or should be written on a separate piece of acid free cloth tape and stitched with a needle and thread. Every small care has to be taken that objects are not harmed in any way by such acts.

3. Faulty repair methods such as use of cellotape, glue tapes, adhesive tapes or any other untested material should not be used on the object. Care has to be taken that added material has the required

compatibility and as far as possible reversible in composition. Repairs are not to be attempted by Curators since it is the speciality of a Conservation Scientist.

4. Monitoring of various parameters of environment has to be done regularly and for the study of round the clock measurement of various factors so that preventive measures could be devised accordingly. This includes temperature, relative humidity, light intensity, U.V. radiations and pollutants.

5. Proper management of the movement of objects within various sections of the museum, their handling technology has to be formulated. Use of a trolly, a fork lift and other mechanized devices should be used.

6. Safe storage has to be planned according to the material and individual objects. We should not dump objects, overcrowding to be stopped and specialized stores to be devised for painting, textiles, manuscripts etc.

8. Proper planning for fire protection and disaster planning has to be done after careful consideration of all aspects and nature of collections. In museums water based fire extinguishers have to be discarded since these would destroy the organic collection.

9. Condition of artifacts at the time of entry into a collection and at regular intervals to be monitored so as to study the decaying process to understand the mechanism of decay. This should be repeated as frequently as possible depending on the magnitude of their collection and infrastructure at the command of a particular museum. Every year recording of such observation would help immensely.

10. Documentation of artifacts such as textual, graphic and photographic has to be done for all objects in the collection. Computer (Optical Disc facility) has to be used for proper assessment of the situation and retrieval of the information on them. Documentation has to be faithful. Major museums can make a beginning in this regard.

11. Collective responsibility and accountability for the safety of the collection has to be ensured not only for security reasons but also from conservation point of view.

12. Proper packing and transportation technology has to be evaluated and adopted for the overall management and movement of the objects for smooth functioning and safety in the working of a museum.

13. The materials used for making display cases has to be such so that they do not promote decay of exhibits in any case. Compatibility is a must.

14. Fumigation at the time of mixing new objects with old collections has to be done to check any possible infection. Modern fumigation techniques using environment friendly methods to be used.

15. Clean dust free surroundings as a measure of good housekeeping to be strictly followed. Vacuum cleaning to be used whereever possible with care. Fragile materials to be handled carefully so as to avoid any damage due to pressure cleaning.

16. Smaller institutions should get in touch with specialists in their region with institutions of National importance. Institutions of National importance could help in this task by providing help.

17. The segregation of damaged objects from objects in good conditions or treated object to be done and in no circumstances these should be mixed with each other because it would make the exercise futile if not followed strictly.

3.3 TRAINING OF CONSERVATION PERSONNEL

Museums today need multidisciplinary approach. Infact every individual working in a museum need specific training in the work which he/she is charged with besides museum management in general. Courses are needed for museologists and historians not only with emphasis on their specialized sphere of activity but conservation technology as per latest thinking so that they can face the challenge of maintaining artifacts in good health for all times to come. The training, therefore, has to be at various levels besides for the conservation staff.

The training of conservation personnel is a complex problem not only in India but even in advanced countries such as U.S.A. On closer examination of the various courses the world over such training courses could be divided into two main categories such as inservice courses and courses for freshers, the former are of shorter duration while the latter are of longer duration. The shorter courses are ranging from 4 weeks to 24 weeks and the longer courses are for a duration of one to five years. However, for the last couple of decades in India emphasis has been on the training of inservice personnel since many of the present day Conservators/Restorers/Chemists did not have a formal longer duration course before their entry into the profession or after entry in service. Such courses have been very useful in boosting up the conservation activities in the country. National Museum, New Delhi, The Govt Museum, Chennai, The National Research Laboratory for Conservation of Cultural Property, Lucknow have been conducting short term courses.

With the creation of more and more laboratories, due to retirement of the first generation conservation personnel and also for the fact that the conservation being more specialised today, it has become necessary to provide persons with longer formal training at the entrance level. In most of the advanced countries, there are training courses which prepare conservation personnel to take up vacant positions. In India, however, the case is reverse. Persons find jobs first and subsequently start knowing about the nature of work they are supposed to attend only after their entry into the service. This many times creates problems besides being a method adopted in those days when people had no other alternatives. This is no more desirable now.

Many institutions connected with cultural property in India do not have laboratories of their own and, therefore, the objects in their collection suffer decay. Trained persons, to take up position in these institutions as well as to fill the vacant position whereever needed, are lacking and, therefore, the interest of conservation suffers. The need of the hour, therefore, is to have a planned programme of creating new laboratories and also provision of trained personnel to take up positions in these newly created laboratories or to fill the vacant positions in the old established laboratories. Though the short term courses have been able to cater to the needs of laboratories, as regards personnel this is not enough for a developing country like India where conservation movement is still getting to its full gear. The obvious choice, therefore, is to train freshers preferably graduates (Science/Fine Arts) for a longer period of 2-3 years in order to fully expose them to jobs they are to attend after training.

(A) Scope

In India cultural properties are being looked after by the Archaeological Survey of India, State Archaeology departments, National Museums, Museums of National importance, State Museums, National Gallery of Modern Art,

Museums and similar institutions, National Archives of India, National Research Laboratory for conservation of Cultural Property and the National Museum of Natural History etc. The material that is being conserved by these institutions is of varied nature and, therefore, it is very difficult to find a common course content for all of them. Emphasis has to be on a general course content followed by specialised training according to individual needs, besides internship for a year or so with a major institution.

This would give the trainees sufficient exposure in order to take up vacant positions in the field. The scope of such a teaching should depend on the needs of the materials connected with archaeology, museums, archives and picture galleries. A student who completes such a course content should be able to stand to the requirements of today. This course would lead them to a degree of post graduate level and later induce them for doctorate studies in the filed of conservation. Such a course would provide confidence to the students and the authorities so that they could safely entrust their objects to them for conservation. No one institution can take up such a course in isolation and, therefore, there ought to be a collaborative attempt. However, the general teaching has to be at one place followed by specialised teaching according to individual needs. There should be arrangements for completion of the training of their choice and field of specialisation. The course should cover history of materials, material science, construction techniques of works, conservation techniques, theory and practice according to scientific methodology. Such a training could lead the students to be real professionals in the field.

(B) Solution

The most appropriate solution is to have an institute to be called the 'Conservation Centre' which should be near larger teaching faculty, a large museum, archives or a library cum documentation centre. The conservation centre should have sufficient floor area nearly 20,000 sq ft to provide for laboratories, class and seminar rooms. Teachers with good academic back ground and long experience in the field should be appointed on a competitive salary to attract talent, besides, Visiting Faculty Teachers should be invited to teach their field of specialized subject.

During first year a solid foundation could be established in the nature of all major types of materials used for the construction and repair of works of art, textiles, books and manuscripts including course on art, history, technology and structure of works of Arts, materials of art and archaeology and environmental effects.. The second year could be devoted to series of lectures, laboratory courses devoted to various organic and inorganic materials. The last six months of the second year could cover the respective fields of specialisation with more emphasis on practice of conservation restoration. For the final year the students may be attached to an institution of their choice as internes either in the country or abroad. Degree should be awarded only after successful completion and a detailed evaluation of the theoretical as well as practical competence of the candidates.

(C) Syllabus

First Semester

1. General Study

(a) Introduction to the subject

(b) Introduction to various materials

(c) Introduction to history of Art

(d) General problems of preservation in relation to the agencies of deterioration

(e) Study of the working of a museum and its laboratory including packing and transport of objects.

2. **Environment and Atmospheric Chemistry**

   (a) Definitions

   (b) Study of various parameters

   (c) Damage caused due to environmental factors including light.

   (d) Air pollution and material change

   (e) Control methods and monitoring of pollutants

3. **Biological factors of decay**

   (a) Micro-organisms

   (b) Insects

   (c) Rodents

   (d) Preventive methods of control

   (e) Curative methods of control

4. **Physical Deterioration**

   (a) Packing and transport of art objects from preservation point of view

   (b) Storage of art collection from preservation angle

   (c) Handling of objects to deter damage

   (d) Display of art objects from preservation point of view

5. **Practicals**

   (a) Measurement of temperature, relative humidity visible and U.V.light

(b) Control of light and U.V. radiation, temperature and humidity

(c) Identification of micro-organism and insects

(d) Packing and transport of art objects

(e) Display and storage of various materials.

Second Semester

6. Detailed study of source material

(a) Objects (Inorganic/organic)

(b) Paintings (Traditional/western)

(c) Paper (Manuscripts/Books/Archival materials)

(d) Textile collections

(e) Ethnographic collection.

7. Structure of Artifacts and Method of their making

(a) Objects (Inorganic/organic)

(b) Paintings (Traditional/western)

(c) Paper (Manuscripts/Books/Archival materials)

(d) Textiles collection

(e) Ethnographic collection.

8. Deterioration

(a) Objects (Inorganic/organic)

(b) Paintings (Traditional/western)

(c) Paper (Manuscripts/Books/Archival materials)

(d) Textile collection

(e) Ethnographic collection.

9. Conservation Techniques-practicals

(a) Objects (Inorganic/organic)

(b) Paintings (Traditional Western)

(c) Paper (Manuscripts/Books/archival materials)

(d) Textile Collection

(e) Ethnographic collection

10. Area of Specialisation

(a) Analysis of material and problems

(b) Introduction and use of different materials for conservation

(c) Introduction of equipments for investigation of defects

(d) Introduction of equipments for conservation

(e) Evaluation of various conservation techniques.

11. Practical work

(a) Conservation under the guidance of the course supervisor

(b) Display and storage

(c) The effects of time on the originality

(d) Effects of conservation treatment

(e) Visit to the workshop of artists in the specified field.

12. Photography and Documentation

(a) Black & white photography and preparation of reports.

(b) Colour slides

(c) UV and IR photography

(d) X-ray

(e) Microphotography & macrophotography

(f) Practicals in photography

13. Practical Conservation

(a) Independent case study of at least two types of objects (one specified and one any other).

(b) Preparation of conservation report

(c) Proposed treatment

(d) Actual conservation

(e) Evaluation

Fourth Semester

14. Internship at the Institute of specialisation in the country or abroad.

15. Final Examination :

Theory & Practical

(D) Training of Conservator/Restorers

The profession of conservation/restoration is still undefined in India. Theie are departments which even today continue with the designations relevant to the situation five decades back such as a Chemist. A Chemist is basically charged with the responsibilities of analysis of materials, alteration products and knowledge of chemicals, reagents, preservatives including their interaction with the art works. But the basic question is who has to apply the knowledge thus gained to the art objects with the aim of restoring them. More often he/she is not the person who has to carry out the conservation also since a person suitable for analytical work may not be as well suitable for the restoration work. In many laboratories, therefore, the actual conservation is done by the Conservation/Restoration Technician or at times by a skilled Attendant only. The results thus may not be the same if this work was done by the trained Conservator/Restorer who has professional skills besides theoretical knowledge of what is being done and why. Simple supervision in the former case would not help and results may be disastrous if not immediately then in the long run.

A Conservator/Restorer should be allowed practice only if one has undergone a thorough training in the study of the methods of making art objects, nature of materials, mechanism of their interaction with the environment and the deteriorating agencies, knowledge of the behavior of chemicals, consolidants and preservatives with the art works. He/she should have a deep understanding of the problems and how to take care of them successfully. Conservator/Restorers dealing with museums of science and technology or museums of natural history/sciences have special needs and they should not rely on persons trained in technique of industrial maintenance only or commercial taxidermists respectively. People in conservation profession should also realise the importance of their work and compare them with professions such as those of Physicians, Engineers and Architects who have passed a phase of self examination and have established widely accepted standards on the basis of thorough training and even internship in their respective fields before they enter the conservation/restoration profession. Organisations such as IASC may think of issuing licences to persons desirous of starting practice, as is done in other professional fields mentioned above by their respective organisations so that professional ethics could be established.

3.4. ART HERITAGE AND TOURISM

To preserve our large inheritance the various concerned agencies require infrastructure and adequate funds which could come from governmental or non-governmental sources. It is said that culture can serve as a tool for diplomacy and a money spinner when tourism and culture go hand in hand. Tourism, therefore, can also generate resources with which the cultural heritage can be adequately managed and conserved. The help from various business houses, as it is in vogue abroad, is yet to come in India for conserving out cultural wealth. Everybody be rest assured that money spent on conservation of our heritage is actually an investment for a noble cause.

Promotion of tourism has become essential as it could bring additional resources including the much needed revenue which could be used for development. Conservation of our past heritage by the government even after 55 years of sustained efforts, has remained inadequate. It is needless to mention that the budget allocations for cultural management have remained disproportionate to our actual needs as an independent Nation even though ours is one of the very ancient civilisation. Every year around the country, a large number of people visit museums, historic monuments and ancient sites to make contact with the past. Further mobilisation of tourism to enhance resources and show our cultural holdings to as many people as we can, is the need of the hour. It would certainly increase the number of visitors but this increasing number of visitors without adequately planning for the infrastructure needed to meet the challenge could prove detrimental to our heritage. It is thus necessary to control the access of visitors to some extent to safeguard the structures and the art objects. Existing visitation statistics need to be reviewed. It is imperative to integrate tourism planning work with the conservation planning process.

Vandalism and negligence were not only confined to the past but continue even today. A sense of apathy, disrespect and indifference among the populous towards our monuments and museum artifacts stems from their not understanding the significance of these structures and art objects in their day to day life. The challenge today is to educate, create awareness and induce a sense of ownership and pride among the people of their cultural heritage. Cultural tourism, therefore, needs a cautious approach based on scientific study of the physical, chemical, biological and mechanical impact on our ancient relics and how they as citizens can contribute to the preservation and up keep of their cultural heritage so crucial for its survival for posterity to see and cherish. It is certainly not the only job of a Conservator but of collective efforts from all quarters of the society.

(A) Problem

Studies show that every visitor who enters a museum or a monument and remains there for about 15-20 minutes, leaves about 20 gms. water (vapour) in the enclosed area resulting into fluctuations of relative humidity which accelerate chemical decay. The large number of tourists are thus responsible for inducing physical decay in terms of abrasion resulting into erosion caused by foot steps of visitors walking on the base structure of a monument every day. Sometimes they stand with their backs using painted walls as a support causing physical loss of painted areas. The growth of biogens contribute decay significantly by large number of visitors. Bacteria brought by them would promote biodegradation especially on painted plaster or soft calcium carbonate structures changing it chemically if the limit crosses the permissible parameters. Also touching of the walls, exhibits, marble screens, stairs and other accessible portions of delicate structures would accumulate uniform layer of grease, oil and dirt, blackening them .It, thus becomes a recurring problem which needs attention. Splashes of *"PAN"* etc. can also be seen at many places.

The museums, the protected buildings and other repositories of the cultural heritage are also not safe and are easily approachable for such damaging acts out of ignorance, neglect and lack of respect for the cultural relics, resulting into disfigurement or destruction of the cultural assets. Such acts are not confined to the developing countries alone : *Fiesta* by Michelangelo, was severely damaged by hammer blows in St. Peter's Cathedral in Rome. Rubens *Descent into Hell* was disfigured by throwing a solvent on it in Munich and Rembrandt's *Nightwatch* in Rijksmuseum, Amsterdam was slit with a knife. These acts are not confined to persons of unsound mind only but can be attributed to fanatics of different types.

There are innumerable examples of exhibition visitors doing minor damages to displayed objects (Plate 7) by touching them especially the private parts of the images in our country; scribbling their names, etc. on museum objects with ball pens, pencils and at times with anything harder than the material of the art object. These can be seen on any monument and old building spread over a large area. This practice has to be stopped forthwith.

The menace of scribing the names of their near and dear one's is often noticed on artifacts or on the monument walls painted or otherwise. This shows general tendency of people at large and lack of conern for these relics of the past. On the other hand measures like flood-lighting sometimes when beyond limits may damage the monument scientifically/aesthetically. The increase in tourism as such, is an encouraging aspect but the steep torrent of visitors only to a few select monuments has its own problems. This is clearly evident in respect of monuments under the World Heritage Series. The number of visitors increase season wise and whenever some special occasions arise, thus increasing the dust carried by the visitors. This accelerates growth of bioactivities also besides making the place unhygienic.

Museum exhibits are also prone to touching by visitors and at times showing disrespect towards them. Sometimes inadvertently people touch the feet of a particular image thus making it dirty and could result in abrading it physically. Over-crowding may result into accidently breaking the sculpture exhibited in an open gallery (Plate 8) space on a pedestal. In monuments some areas may become structurally weak thus needing extra care.

(B) Proposed Steps

Conservation measures today must pioneer a new relationship between the people and their cultural heritage and instill in them a sense of ownership. Movement of the visiting public should be restricted to outside the halls of the monuments thus helping prevent the unintentional misuse and vandalism of the premises. Since the development in the ambience around the monuments and museums and the visitors vis-a-vis the development will have to coexist, it would be appropriate to create a sort of 'Buffer Zone' at visiting places to mitigate the direct impact on the structure and exhibits. The movement of visitors could thus be regulated in such a manner that their impact could be managed to minimum levels at a time. The flow of visitors should be monitored and controlled accordingly. Audio-visuals could be shown at different locations to control the visitor movement.

Such an attempt to impose limits on the number of people allowed entry at a given time often elicit immediate negative reactions from the interested groups. Cultural management authorities and tourism authorities often work independently and this disjunction may create conflicts of interest as tourism authorities may like to bring more and more people to monuments and museums. They often forget the physical impact of large numbers of visitors on ancient structures/buildings and artifacts. The need, therefore, is of planning and management of places to manage the large number of people, has to be well thought of for a proper administration of places of interest. There should be a dichotomy between the preservation of heritage and tourism. Economics of resources thus gathered should be used primarily for conservation and also for better management of sites and museums to ensure safety of artifacts and visitor relationship. Adequate planning of the interaction of the two has to be given due consideration before a decision to enhance tourism is taken. The infrastructure at these places in terms of manpower has to be provided proportionately to regulate visitor movement and also monitor their actions while visiting these places of interest. Some areas could also be kept out of the reach of the visitors, flow of visitors could be channelised and adequate guide programmes/visuals should be planned in such a way that the mechanical impact of visitors is restricted to minimum.

(C) Experiences of some other Countries

Giorgio Torraca presented a paper as back as 1968 at the National Seminar on conservation of Cultural Property organised by the Indian Association for the Study of Conservation of Cultural Property in India on "Relation of Relative Humidity to Wall Paintings Preserved under ground level" in three countries namely, Italy, France and Bulgaria. Experience of Tarquinia Italy-Etouscan Tombs with Mural Paintings shows that R.H.-is above 93% in nonvisited closed tombs. Holes were pierced in the doors to allow ventilation. Nonvisited tombs kept well while visited ones show sign of deterioration namely efflorescences of Calcium carbonate and loss of cohesion of plaster. No biological Fungi / Bacteria were noticed. Here visitors are allowed in small groups 10-20 persons.

In summer condensation of water on tomb walls is most likely to happen when temperature drops back to normal after visits. In any season the R.H. decreases during visits, must cause evaporation of water from the walls. Since this water contains Calcium bicarbonate, it leaves behind on evaporation efflorescence of Calcium carbonate which can damage the paint layer. Carbon-di-oxide produced by visitors remain inside the tombs, being heavier than air and is dissolved in water contained in the walls. Water which now contains carbon-di-oxide can dissolve Calcium carbonate through formation of soluble bicarbonate. This process can damage the surface of the walls & the mural paintings. Other volatile acids produced by the visitors can also be brought to the surface of the walls by condensation of humidity. Therefore, allowing only a small number of visitors at one time, reduction of the number of tombs visited by a single visitor can go a longway to save these cultural relics and if need be, they can even be closed for visitors.

Since our attempts to attract more and more visitors to our cultural institutions is a welcome step yet caution is the *'Mantra'* which would go a longway in preserving the murals etc. for posterity.

3.5. DISASTER PLANNING FOR MUSEUMS

India suffers from three major natural calamities year after year in one part of the country or the other resulting into loss of valuable lives and property. It is true that at present the technology to forecast floods, cyclones and earthquakes has yet to be perfected, especially in case of earthquakes. No amount of relief work can restore back the lives lost. Similarly no amount of restoration/conservation efforts can bring back the originality of artifacts once these are affected by these calamities. Protection of our cultural heritage which is vested in the organisations for the society against natural disasters, falls within the field of conservation studies. Prevention of decay or damage is the highest form of conservation. Three main disasters are as follows.

(a) Fire

(b) Flood

(c) Earthquake

These can also be classified as :

(i) Man-made

(ii) Natural

(A) Fire

(a) Ordinary Combustible Material — Wood, Paper, Textiles etc.

(b) Inflammable Materials — Oil, Grease, Organic Chemicals etc.

(c) Electrical Installations

Fire is one of the most devastating causes of mass destruction of all materials whether inorganic in nature like stone, ceramics, metals or of organic in composition such as wood, paper, cloth etc. Art objects and library materials especially being organic in nature can get reduced to ash in no time if adequate precautions are not taken to prevent fire in the buildings housing them. Fire could be local or could spread eventually over a large area on one floor or could spread to several galleries or stack areas even on different floors. All fires in the beginning would be local and would spread to adjoining areas but in case it is due to inflammable materials or electric short circuit, it could spread very very quickly and could become unmanageable. There are instances when fire has destroyed valuable art collections, records, books or even people, if trapped inside a building where fire has broken out.

Fire has a great potential to destroy materials quickly and therefore, its destructive powers need to be understood and managed accordingly. For elimination of fires we need to devise a technology involving three distinct steps namely i.e.

(i) prevention

(ii) detection and

(iii) extinction.

Prevention

It could be either passive or active type. Passive measures which are preventive in character include facilities for quenching the fire by water hydrants at easy approachable locations, use of fire resistant materials especially for interiors, provision for doors etc. so that the fire from one area does not spread to the other areas easily and could be contained within the space where it started, separate exists for evacuation of people trapped inside and use of good quality electric fittings of durable and standard installations to avoid unnecessary heating especially of the incandasent spot lights and lamps.

Besides these measures it could be ensured that laboratory and other workshops should be far from the galleries/stack areas and stores. Care has to be taken that combustible goods such as packing cases, packing materials, discarded furnitures, waste materials should be stored well away from the main building and last but not the least smoking should be strictly prohibited inside museums and libraries. Constant monitoring of the electrical installations should be done periodically to check heating which tends to weaken insulations of the electric wiring after some use. In case the institution has a conservation laboratory of its own, it needs special arrangements to prevent fire since this is the place where combustible chemicals are being used regularly which are a great fire hazard. As regards active measures to prevent fire are concerned, these include fire detection and extinction, if need be. However, museum and libraries contain easily perishable materials and, therefore, they need special care to detect and eventually extinguish the fire, if any.

Detection

Immediate detection of fire is of utmost importance so as to take action to extinguish it quickly before it is too late and becomes unmanageable. It could be detected by constant vigilance and continuous monitoring of the various areas by security staff. However, during the period when these areas, having valuable materials, are closed especially at night this work can be done by automatic alarms which could detect fire as soon as it starts. The detection system are of various kinds such as

(i) Heat detectors

(ii) Smoke detectors

(iii) Flame detectors

(iv) Radiant energy detectors

(v) Laser beam detectors which is the latest in the filed of fire detection.

These detectors make the automatic alarm systems active to indicate fire or possibilities of fire. Very often the alarm system automatically makes the fire extinguishing system operative to take care of the fire. Generally these are two types which work on the use of water sprinklers or production of gas engulfing systems to start automatically. For the museums and libraries the latter type are most suited as water sprinkling systems would certainly extinguish the fire but would damage further the organic materials resulting into their total destruction. Many a times due to lack of proper knowledge much damages could happen unintentionally. It is, therefore, necessary to know about these specific fire extinguishing methods suited for museums and libraries in order to avoid any consequent damage out of ignorance and fear of possible damage to adjoining areas. These alarm systems also need constant inspection, routine testing of their functioning to ensure that at times of need they would not fail but help in detection quickly. Laser beam detectors are very sensitive and can sense fire from a distance of as much as 100 meters and are sensitive to heat and smoke both making them most effective.

Extinction

Even though the help of a fire brigade is available, particularly in large cities these days, it is essential to have museum and library personnel some knowledge of the fire fighting apparatus and how to use them as per needs of the particular collection. Fires are classified as under. While using fire fighting equipments one needs to know what to use and how to use them.

1. Fire involving ordinary combustible material e.g. wood, paper, textiles etc
2. Fire involving inflammable materials such as organic chemicals, oil, grease etc
3. Fire involving electrical installations such as short circuiting.

First step, therefore, is to identify the type of fire because on it would depend the use of a particular type of fire extinguisher. Fire extinguishers are of various types.

1. Foam type gives a thick foam which covers the area of the fire and cuts off the oxygen supply on fire. Suited for fires due to electric faults and fire of oil etc.

2. Soda Acid type gives a powerful stream of water due to action of acid on the soda. This is not suited for museum and libraries of organic nature but for other types it could be used.

3. CTC type uses carbon tetrachloride which is vaporized into gas and can be used in museum and libraries but it is toxic in nature.

4. Carbon dioxide type is useful for museums and libraries.

5. Dry chemical type where chemicals in dry powder form are used to extinguish fires of all types as they adhere to the heated surfaces.

6. Halongenated hydrocarbonates are very much in use these days and are very effective in all type of fires.

One of these is Halon Gas (C Br Cl F_2) which is Bromo chloro difluoro methane. It extinguishes fire by inhibiting the chemical reaction of fuel and oxygen. These are based on two main principles of total flooding and local flooding. While the last type fire extinguishing system needs the in-built structural installations but all others are portable and manual. These should be kept at conspicuous places and personnel working in museums and libraries should be got trained in the use of those extinguishers which are suitable for museums and libraries so that the fires before becoming real dangers could be extinguished.

The foam type and soda acid type are not suitable for museums and libraries but carbon dioxide type, dry chemical type, CTC type are most effective where organic objects are stored. The fire fighting equipments need to be inspected periodically and should be recharged on the dates recommended by the manufactures as the chemicals inside them do not remain effective indefinitely.

Prevention of fire, therefore, is of great importance for museums and libraries. Fire hazards must be studied in totality in order that all museums and library personnel understand the potential dangers so that their occurrences may be eliminated entirely or reduced to the extent possible. Portable fire extinguishers are handy but their working should be made clear to all concerned. The best suited, however in a building being planned, is to instal automatic alarm system coupled with the fire extinguishing systems room wise so that the fires could be checked before these become potential dangers for the collections. Fire brigade services are available in most of the cities these days but contact should be made with them so that suitable fire fighting technology could be planned and installed which would suit the specific requirements of the museum and libraries.

Planning of the building in such a manner that it is equipped for protection against fire. Doors, separation of one gallery from the other in order to contain it within the place where it has started, separate exit for evacuation of visitors and staff, provision for water hydrants, fire extinguishers, labs to be away from the galleries, electric installations must be of the best quality, fire resistant materials to be used in stores and galleries, constant checking of the electrical installations especially spot lights, materials such as packing cases, padding material, discarded furniture, waste material should be stored away from the store and galleries and precaution such as no smoking should be allowed in the galleries, stores, packing area and laboratory to avoid any mishap.

(B) Flood

Location of Museums, Libraries etc.

(a) These buildings should be well away from river banks or flood prone area.

(b) These should not be in low lying areas where accumulation of rain water in case of heavy rains or cloud burst could be potential source.

(c) Near the sea where in case of a cyclones, tidal wave rise could allow water to come inside the buildings.

(d) Drainage systems should be checked regularly for any leakage seeping inside the building.

(e) Over head water storage tanks for water supply or air conditioning cooling plant has to be regularly inspected for any water seepage.

(f) Materials such as paper, paintings, textiles and other organic materials should not be displayed on the ground floor or basement.

Prevention measures

(1) Flood affected materials should not be allowed to dry too quickly and in no case we should try to open them up after drying is complete.

(2) Drying should be in controlled chambers.

(3) Freeze drying has a great potential and, therefore, materials in wet condition should be taken to such a facility to be handled by experts.

The theory that prevention is better than cure is correct, but it is difficult to apply, human nature being what it is. We all hope and pray that a disaster won't happen, and we all go about our business of caring for cultural heritage without developing the management techniques to make it in people's interest to prepare for foreseeable risks. It is true that exact date of an earthquake could not have been predicted but had the strengthening measures been applied in advance to our museum buildings wherein most of the artifacts are housed or exhibited could have been saved. There are cycles of intense earthquakes such as the one in Gujarat during January 2001 and there after the last was on 26th-27th January 2002 even though of mild intensity. Damage to Bhuj Museum building Gujarat and the artifacts on the first floor gallery is the latest example.

Govt of India took measures for compiling a Vulnerability atlas of India to study the matter at length. However, preventive measures needed to be taken remain in the books only as regards museum buildings are concerned since museum in general and conservation in particular often have a very low priority. It is true that many important museums in India fall in the high risk zones where earthquakes could inflict heavy damage to them. Unfortunately even though there is a great damage potential especially from seismic disturbances to Indian museums no substantial efforts to take care of these have been made even after five decades of our independence.

(C) Earthquake

The whole of India is divided in 'five seismic zones ranging from very high risk zone to no risk zone'. A large majority of our museums in India are prone to seismic risks of varied intensity on Richter scale. Baring a few museums almost all major museums in India are falling in high risk areas and moderate risk areas. The fear, therefore, overshadows museums at New

Delhi, Patna, Simla, Mumbai, Bhubaneshwar, Chennai, Panjim, Trivandrum and Guwahati to name a few. We should study which museum building has provisions to make them seismic resistant and which is not safe as yet. This would help museums to take preventive measures on priority basis to make them seismic resistant without waiting for fresh tremors to come and inflict irreparable damage to our cultural wealth.

Geo-chemical anomalies in the soil show that the matter is an active fault in the earth's structure because the ***Tectonic*** plates of the subcontinent are indeed pushing against Asia and over millions of years such faults may very well have developed in the earth's crust. However, as and when the faults become destabilized because of the energy which has remained suppressed could create new stress zones resulting into more tremors in future which cannot be predicted precisely as to when these would come. Secondly whether the storage cases, pedestals of artifacts and showcases in our museums are having measures to cope with the tremors. As far as known to me there are no such provisions and, therefore, we need to develop a rational seismic retrofitting policy for our museum buildings. It is also believed that buildings in general on a rocky underground are more safe comparatively. Deep digging into the earth also helps in activating the seismic faults in the earth. In some cases high rise buildings at the same location differed in their response to the earthquake in Gujarat recently. Some have come down whereas a few could stand the tremors of 6.9 on Rikter scale for obvious reasons. It could be inferred that the supervising and certifying agencies did not adhere to the codes as to make easy money in connivance with the builders to reduce the cost of construction. Advice of seismic experts was not adhered to maintain safety guidelines chalked out by them. The net result of all the above has created the`confusing situation and loss of precious life and property including the culture heritage. There is also a tendency of taking things very casually and unless some people in the government machinery are made responsible/accountable for the lapse, things would hardly improve. Newspapers are reporting about possible great risks of damage due to earthquake atleast in North India.

Preventive measures

It is time to think that in India preventive measures have not been planned in advance to meet such challenges and, therefore, lot of efforts need to be taken to rehabilitate and rebuild the damages to provide relief to victims after the calamity which takes a long time to come to pre earthquake situation besides a large extra burden on the exchequers. The actual need of the hour, therefore, is to understand the potential danger of these calamities and remain ever vigilant to face any such situations by taking appropriate preventive measures so as to minimise the future damages to property of all types and loss of innocent lives. In connection with the cultural property damages it can be said that cent percent restoration of these artifacts can never retrieve them back to their original physical state, their asthetics, their beauty and excellence.

(a) For buildings

It is reported that the art of designing to resist earthquakes is still not fully developed using codes based on gross simplifications with horizontal loadings or base sharing as the design criteria for new buildings, but such codes can not be applied to historic buildings which are of a different structure typology. Many museum buildings such as the Govt Museum, Chennai and Indian Museum, Kolkata besides a few more are historic in nature now since some of them have completed even 150 years recently. The seismic spectrum would depend on soil types, the slope of sedimentary soils, the existence of any bedding planes and their angle of slope, horizontal changes in soil type, the depth of the soil over bedrock and the topography of the bedrock 'including ridges and deposited soil (Dowrick, 1977). In 1989 a quake rocked California and San Francisco. A 49 story office building shook for more than a minute and the top floor swayed more than one foot from side to side. However, no damage was reported. This was possible because California has the strictest building codes when comes to earthquake preparedness. This shows that technology is there which needs to be followed. In smaller place like Uttarkashi and Chamoli many houses 100-150 years old have survived the earthquakes. Thus there is also a need to look into the traditional construction techniques. Use of reinforcing lintel bands, strengthening corridors, smaller openings, corner bracing, light roof are some of the basic characteristics of these houses that have survived the earthquakes. There are, therefore, traditional methods which could be studied in detail since old structures have survived several quakes in the hills of Utaranchal over the centuries.

Several other measures have been suggested world over. All existing museum buildings require some modifications and strengthening as per earthquake resistant designs. For this purpose more amount of steel and certain specific load sharing/bearing pillars are required, Those would ensure that the horizontal forces created by an earthquake do not lead to a collapse. To withstand an earthquake a structure needs to be bound properly so that it could act as a whole mass and not separate components. During an earthquake all buildings sway but the ones which are bound properly remain intact. "The key lies in strengthening the joints between the vertical columns and horizontal beams around which a reinforced cement and concrete structure is built" says a Delhi Architect Arjun Thapar. Base isolation technique has been used in U.S.A. in some buildings. It is reported that during 1994 quake that rocked Los Angeles, a hospital built with this technique survived the quake despite being very near to the epicenter. Prestressed concrete structure can sustain shocks of earthquakes which are being used to build flyovers, overhead rail tracks these days. But our problem is how to introduce this technology in old museum buildings and hence the need for an alternate technology which can resist the seismic shocks which museum artifacts would experience at the time of seismic tremors in times to come. In fact building bye-laws prescribe the insertion of an earthquake proof band at the sill level to make them vibration resistant. Japan these days uses steel-reinforced housing using contemporary quake resistant technologies which survived comparatively well. Japanese seismic engineering expertise remains the best in the world but the latest major earthquake at Kobe has forced them to collaborate with their counterparts from U.S.A. Floating foundation instead of running the foundation supports deep, a multitude of short concrete piling can be driven into the soil under the raft. The building can be divided into sections so that it could 'bob' during the quake and the entire weight of the building can be supported on a cushion foundation. It has also been suggested to use hollow bricks and special treatment of the foundation among the steps that can help a building absorb the shocks of a quake. All this has become necessary because of man's increasing pressure and intervention especially at the fault lines.

(b) Museum Interiors

The possibility of damage to fragile objects on display/storage in museums during an earthquake is significant even if the building structure itself remains intact. Violent shaking and tilting of rigid structures can lead to object overturn, fracture resulting from dynamic loading stresses or sliding and collision of the object with neighboring objects or walls. The display system commonly used in a museum are either floor mounted or pedestal mounted or case mounted or suspended or wall mounted. Each of these mountings require analysis of the non-structured component and of the primary structure system supporting that component. The problem is complex. Before any specific type of fixtures are suggested we have to first establish the nature of the display and the profiles of the artifacts displayed (flexible, rigid, hard, soft, heavy, brittle, ductile etc). Next is to establish the display concept, the type of support, the type of mounting. The next step is most significant that of establishing the relationship between the response of the structural system and the artifact mounting. This must be clearly defined and the instructions understood. Both the artifact and its mounting needs to be reviewed to define whether sliding, overturning, rocking or yielding will occur. It may be necessary to perform dynamic testing to discover the answer.

California is an earthquake prone country. The J.Paul Getty Museum is near six earthquake faults and, therefore, experiences tremors more frequently. Bob Nicbore at the University of Southern California used computer models to study the seismic vibrations to measure their impact on displayed objects. Based on this study he recreated the earthquake movements/shocks in the laboratory. They tried to find out how much movement the displayed objects in J.Paul Getty Museum can tolerate that would keep the objects stationery during actual earthquake. The concept was simple. The base of the object was provided with springs that would keep absorbing the shocks which in turn would keep the object stationary from the tremors. Large statues in their museum faced special problem. Ball bearings were attached to the base of the heavy bronzes and nylon fishline restricts the movement of the mount to the table top. They are also providing special bases to take care the earthquake movements and its likely breakage. This is being done for each sculpture. Every device has to be tailor made.

At the base of the pedestal there is a unit of springs and ball bearings that moves on a concave disc. During the earthquake the springs would expand and contract to absorb the vibrations because its movement is limited to the dimension of the disc and the statue would return to its original position preventing the damage. Seismic engineer help was taken to model these pedestals which could absorb the vibrations whenever these occurred. Every individual object which was stannding on a pedestal or was displayed in a horizontal showcase was provided with these special mounts, the experiences were quite rewarding. The unique aspect in this undertaking is the realization that protection of artifacts is the new goal and that the normal structure engineering procedures which are life-safety oriented are not appropriate. State-of the-art analytical techniques and innovative structural and display systems are required.

With the recent heightened interest in development of disaster mitigation plans for cultural property, the protection of art objects in museums located in seismically active zones has recently emerged as a problem of considerable concern. It is high time we should identify museums most prone to seismic damages and provide preventive measures accordingly. Architects, Civil Engineers, Builders. Museologists and Conservation Scientists should all sit together and chalk-out a policy in this regard while planning new museum buildings but it is also very necessary to discuss as to how an old museum building can even now be provided with structures strengthening to make them earth quake resistant, if not seismic proof. These measures should be planned in such a way that there is minimal damage from seismic shocks to the museum buildings and also protect the artifacts from tremors housed in these buildings by taking an overall remodelling of our display and storage techniques. A methodology has to be worked out to reduce the threat to our displayed/ stored objects from seismic damage. Dr M.S. Mathews, Professor of Civil Engineering, IIT Madras, has recently studied the Rehabilitation and Retrofit of Earthquake damaged monuments in Gujarat. He has stated that there are several antiseismic techniques developed in Italy and Germany which could be studied in relation to Indian conditions. There is a need to adopt and adapt these antiseismic retrofit and rehabilitation techniques to condition in India.

Earthquakes often lead to secondary disasters, such as floods and fire, which can destroy artifacts even though the ground shaking *per se* may not. Broken dams and water pipes release unwanted water and overturned fixtures can lead to fire and can damage the electrical systems. Fire fighting systems may be destroyed by earthquake shaking and that routes of access to fires may be blocked. Another hazard is theft during the confused state of events following a major earthquake. The government agencies, therefore, have to act quickly to meet any such situation before it is too late. It is, therefore, a complex problem which has to be understood in right perspective so that the heritage that the individuals and organizations hold for the society in trust may be safeguarded for future generation to see and enjoy, Preparedness, mitigation, response and recovery are some basic issues which have to be addressed in this direction effectively, as quickly as possible and minimising further damage after such a disaster.

CHAPTER IV

Authenticity and Faking

4.1 AUTHENTICATION

Art works and antiquities recovered from excavations have clues for definite authentication. But today with the emergence of the art dealer the art purchases by museum become doubtful since they very seldom disclose the source of the art works being offered by them for acquisition. The quality of art works being offered by art dealers three decades back was far superior to what is being sold by them now. Museum and other allied institutions which purchase art objects today, therefore, are not very sure about the quality and authenticity of the art works being acquired by them. During the recent past a few cases were detected by the National Museum, New Delhi, which is one of the major buyers of art works in the country for its collection. At present, the usual practice of their authentication is based on stylistic/artistic considerations which is decided by the members of the art purchase committees who are museum Directors, Historians, Archaeologists and Museologists–all experts in their fields but it is needless to mention that the Committee does not include any Conservation Scientist who as a matter of fact has dealt more intimately with art objects while undertaking their conservation or scientific study and thus has long exposure with the body of various art objects, apart from the artist who had created them centuries ago. In consequence the examination at the time of acquisition is based on visual scrutiny and the judgement of the eye. The matter is referred to Conservators if the Committee members differ in their judgement and that too is being followed by one or two museums only. As a matter of fact the situation would be altogether different if a Conservator is also on the Committee to assist it as it would also act as a deterrent to art dealers of disrepute. Museums, therefore, should get their collections authenticated as per scientific studies which have developed in the recent past quite significantly. Moreover, museums very often do not insist on acquiring only those art works which are registered with the Archaeological Survey of India under the Antiquities and Art Treasures Act, 1972 out of a fear of the object being smuggled out of the country, since dealers may get more price for them. Moreover, some experts still are in dilemma whether authenticity is a myth or reality. This shows their bent of mind.

In Europe for centuries, reproducing masterpieces was an accepted fact and was widely practised by student artists to polish up their techniques. Indian artists and students of art colleges also followed this practice during British Raj. Often they are taught how to produce antique look on their works. It is reported that the practice of copying later fell into disreputed hands towards the end of the 19th century with the rise of the status conscious elite and emergence on the scene of the art dealers, who are in business for the quick and enormous gains at very little risk. In the Indian context many of the artist families are following their ancestral craft traditions the way these were centuries ago. They very often use the same techniques, materials and even the tools used by their forefathers in their work even today. Governmental agencies also encourage the art traditions to continue by way of revival of art tradition and have, therefore, supported many such projects where it was ensured that the tradition does not become extinct with age or the so called development as such.

(A) Authenticating Objects

The importance of authenticity having been highlighted at the Nara conference on authenticity (1-6 Nov. 1994) museums & cultural institutions have become extra vigilant. Authenticity by definition means state of being true or of truthfully established origin and provenance. Therefore, authenticity of a work of art depends on the relation between the work itself and the place, the Artist or period to which it is attributed. Authenticity can also be defined as of original creative source that sustains and proves itself. It could also be understood as a condition of the heritage resource, legally valid, reliable, original and genuine etc. Authenticity has to be maintained of the existing heritage resources from the past. They will form a reference for future for the relevant issues. In order to keep their authentic creative capacity we need the dynamic, well thought of conservation management and planning. This includes minute examination and documentation made before restoration/replacement, the quantity of replaced parts is minimized, the size, quality and the species of new material are the same as the previous ones, the workmanship is the same, and the report is published after the work, the replacement/restoration would never violate authenticity. On the other hand the provenance of a work of art depends on the place where it has been made and the source from which it has originated. It does not relate to time or period since these may vary. For example a Gupta sculpture may belong to the kingdom of Guptas, which is demarcated geographically but it may be early Gupta or late Gupta. The provenance of an art object, therefore, has to be specific to be various sources of production of Gupta sculptures. The places thus may vary but within that demarcated areas of their kingdom. It could, therefore, be from that region which could be specified accordingly.

The persistence of traditional crafts which are not converted into modern creation is one of the basic reasons of doubtful authenticity. Lack of historical sense leads to belief that using the same material and technique as in the past is a correct way of saving the traditions. But traditional crafts were the authentic expressions of the present. This results into faking which is unfortunately encouraged by mass tourism and demands for artifacts of the past. The permanence of the craft is in itself not enough to safeguard authenticity and hence the problem. Reconstruction is a also very often due to the wrong views of some concerned people who intend their knowledge to be materialized on the object instead of past documentation in the form of drawings or models while conserving the authentic remains without reconstruction, could lead to unfaithful revival. The real notional values of such artifacts stay within the authenticity of the tradition which could be rediscovered, studied, safeguarded and not to be carried away by over enthusiasms.

(B) Problem

There have been cases, where we have not been able to prove quickly that particular stone sculpture or sculptures belong to India especially in the absence of proper documentation records which could prove our legal ownership having claimed their return to India. It is needless to say, that a large number of our heritage in the form of sculptures have not been documented on scientific lines and hence the problem. Authentication of artifacts has to be on the basis of their documentation records prepared for their characterization done on the basis of a detailed technical study which we often term as fingerprinting. Such a study done on a object immediately after its acquisition or discovery through excavation or having been part of a standing monument would be most significant in this endeavour so as to authenticate them initially and be at a later date. It is a huge task considering our vast cultural heritage and sooner we start it, better it would be.

Very often most of the museums rely on stylistic documentation on the basis of personal judgement of Scholars/Curators since they neither have any facility for any in-house documentation nor do they feel its importance making the situation still grave. The textual, graphic and photographic (visible radiation and invisible radiation) documentation has to be completed in respect of each and every artifact in a collection.

Authentication of artifacts has to be on the basis of the documentation records prepared for their characterization done after a detailed technical study which we call fingerprinting. Such a study done on an object immediately after its acquisition for a collection would be most significant in this regard so as to authenticate them initially and also later, if need be. The textual, graphic and photographic (visible and invisible rays) documentation supported by specific observations made on their chemical composition, physical, petro-graphic, metallographic examination, holography, radiology, macrophotographic studies besides SEM studies done to fingerprint their inner structure and other details in between the various components. This would leave no loopholes which could be manipulated to mislead the Scholars, Museologists and Conservation scientists. Any surface deposits of soil etc could also substantiate the claims of ownership on the basis of these. This has also to be supported by specific observations made on their chemical composition, photographic examination, radiology, macrophotographic examination, besides SEM studies done to fingerprint the inner structure crystalographic details including the inclusion in between various crystals, if any. This would leave no loopholes which could be manipulated by fakers to mislead the Scholars, Museologists in general and Conservation Scientists in particular. Any surface deposits of soil etc. inrespect of stone sculptures recovered from excavations could also substantiate the claims of ownership on the basis of the soil composition by comparison of the residual deposits and the soil of the site from where it was recovered.

(C) Scientific Study

Such a scientific study can deter their replacement, later repair in case such a stone object breaks accidently while on display, in storage and/or during transit. It would also help in retrieving them back for the country in case of a theft or smuggling so that their legal ownership could be proved in a court of law. Instances are there when it became very difficult to establish ownership for example Amin Pillars and their provenance etc. which traveled to U.K. and copies were transplanted in their place at situ besides a copy was seized by the customs at Mumbai. It is needless to say that authentication studies has to be done on the objects in situ, at their new location and if possible on the stone at a nearby quarry near the monument/site from which a particular stone artifact has come. I am sure the fakers cannot match all their characteristics and are bound to make mistakes on which we may encash at the time of authentication. This would also monitor their health over the centuries/years and could help in adopting conservation techniques accordingly.

We must prepare petrographic/microphotographic slide collection of known images from a particulars site for comparison and if need be to authenticate these images or prepare a SEM examination records which could be compared with slides of known objects. This could also help in the study of the inner details which a faker cannot match. Chemical composition could also lead to conclusion in this regard if large number of comparison slides are prepared. Such a study could further be supplemented by taking macrophotographs of various parts of the image. Graphic documentation could also record the details on the surface which would be to difficult to match but an expert eye cannot be cheated while comparing the scientific details thus prepared. Exact nature of the stone used in making a particular image cannot be falsified under expert evaluation of the problem.

There are a large number of stone sculpture of which either arms or legs or head are missing such as the Armless torso of Mathura Budha in the collection of National Museum, New Delhi or Standing Budha in Rastrapati Bhawan, New Delhi which look aesthetically perfect even in the present condition. Large scale reconstruction would go against their authenticity and the missing parts may be left as found originally otherwise there is no end of reconstruction which would be misleading art historically and could give rise to falsification. It could also betray the style, period and provenance of the stone image. Reconstruction, therefore, leads to complication such as faking, replacement and deception. It could also betray the historic sense, moral and ethical values of the profession. In short such stone sculpture would never be the same again. Repair/restoration needed for providing physical strength to the object, if reversible, would stand on the grounds of scientific conservation if needed for safe display or storage, repairs which would not affect the authenticity may be considered collectively by all concerned.

The big question is how far we are serious about authenticating our collection specially of stone objects, are our institutions technically ready, financially sound and ethically ready for such a comprehensive project on the basis of their in-house infrastructure or possible collaboration with appropriate scientific institution in the country or aborad. Moreover, even if we have the technical knowhow, do we have the necessary urge for such a study on priority basis. Let us not be caught unaware and wait for such a study till any future mishap actually occurring, when perhaps, it could be too late.

4.2 Finger Printing

Lately a large number of instances have come to light where the simple craftsmen were being exploited by the people in the Art trade to produce fakes and forgeries almost in all types of art works. Even the art works of recent origin were camouflaged very cleverly to look like old and vice versa which gave smuggling of art works a great boost and the illicit trade is rampant today. As per a latest press report Sotheby's, the world famous art auction house have launched its operations in India to develop the market of fine art. They would act as agents for potential buyers and sellers of works of art in this country also. However, it remains to be seen how museums or similar institutions react to this development and how the Sotheby's overcome this skill of the forgers and fakers in India. There are persons in authority who sometimes advocate such sales by Auction houses.

The agencies to check this menance of faking are not adequately equipped for correct and quick detection of such an unethical/unlawful act in the country. To rely on the iconographic or sylistic attributes of an art work is just not enough. One has to go a little deeper to be on a right track. The faker is bound to make a mistake. He might try to do everything right but is bound to commit a mistake like a culprit leaving a clue which is used for detailed investigation by a trained forensic expert from where he could start towards the correct conclusions. Such a study in the context of authentication of art works can be done only by a Conservation Scientist/Conservator/Restorer of long experience and adequately trained for such an investigation by using latest technology available for the purpose. Such a study could also be supplemented with additional information to fingerprint them for future reference. However, it is a time consuming process and we would observe restraints in adding objects unnecessarily to the already large collections of many museums. We should attempt to fill in the gaps rather than duplicating what we already have in the collections. Authorities should not set aside such an act going on at a large scale on one pretext or the other since today the fabrication of art works is going on at a mass scale all over the country. Sooner the better, we realize this hard fact so that museums stop entry of such objects into their collections of genuinely ancient objects. The current practice of acquiring art works for huge prices at the cost of the tax payer has to be reviewed and if these have to be purchased as a policy to revive the dying art and to help the Artisans then such works may be acquired for modern museums and art galleries or craft collections as such objects would also become extinct and rare with time. One has to distinguish between genuinely ancient object and a contemporary work of art.

It is reported that creation of substandard syndrome is a human weakness which even great men of the world could not overcome. According to a story reported elsewhere, Lorenzo de Medica advised Michael Angelo the renowned painter, sculptor and poet of Italy, to pass one of his early sculpture as an ancient work. The Florentine artist accordingly buried his 'Sleeping Cupid' in damp ground and it was allowed to remain there till its surface had run sufficiently stained by the earth and the humidity to give it an appearance of the great age. The sculpture later was sent to an art dealer in Rome. He sold it to a cardinal for 200 ductas paying Michael Angelo 20 ductas out of that for his work. The cardinal was not to be fooled for long. He discovered that the Cupid was a recent work and got his money back. Michael Angelo, however, kept his 20 ductas. Such a practice, therefore, is not new to Europe where now many museums do not acquire unless the art works are thoroughly examined using latest technology by Conservation Specialists prior to acquisition. Besides this, objects are acquired at auctions where these are well documented, authenticated, certified and publicized well before their acquisition by any public institution.

It is hard to believe that the authorities in India are not aware of such a *modus operandi* of art acquisitions abroad. However, they continue authorizing museums to acquire art objects through annual art purchase bazar for reasons better known to them where the time available at the disposal of the experts is very little to decide. Sometimes it looks to be like a February-

March rush of purchases of store items in any Government organisation. This practice if not stopped so far, has to be discontinued immediately.

In the recent past some art works have come back, after being abroad for a decade or so, since these were spotted there after being illegally smuggled out. On their return these were again subjected to visual examination rather than scientifically authenticating them to ensure that only the originals, which went out from the country, have come back now. These could have been very well replaced by duplicates while away. According to a report the Amin Pillars (Plate 9) now in the National Museum, New Delhi were duplicated thrice in India and the authorities were baffled to know which one is the original. Authentication of these could be on surer lines had these been fingerprinted or characterized the moment these were located in the country. In the absence of such a characterization at times it becomes difficult for the owners of these art treasures to establish the identity and the right of ownership of the object. A very serious thought has to be given to this problem, sooner the better by taking scientific parameters as points of reference for the individualization of art works, atleast of those which are of 'National Art Treasurers Category' to start with. The parameters that should necessarily be included for the scientific characterization should be listed and their priorities decided by a team of experts in the country.

It would not be out of place to mention here that one such effort was made a few years back when the National research Laboratory for Conservation of Cultural Property, Lucknow organized a meeting of Scientists and Experts concerned with the efforts of the late Dr. S. Paramasivan to highlight the problem and to decide a course of action as regards antiquities of metal were concerned in which parameters were discussed in depth. The participants came from the Central Forensic Laboratory, Calcutta, the Defence Metallurgical Research Laboratory, Jamshedpur, the National

Museum, New Delhi, the Indira Gandhi Centre for Atomic Research, Kalpakam, experts from A.S.I and the National Research Laboratory for Conservation of Cultural Property, Lucknow besides Dr. Paramasivan. This could be taken up as a National Project if proper follow up is done not only for metal antiquities but for other works of art also after chalking out a well thought of plan project by any agency selected by the Government of India for the purpose. It is, therefore, not only essential to conserve art objects but also to authenticate them so that the future of the past could be ensured and the fear of replacement by fakes could be set aside.

Finger printing of art works and antiquities of all materials could be done if some basic documentation techniques could be used such as Macrophotography, Infra-Red-Photography, Radiology, Elemental analysis along with other physical parameters, use of radioactive isotopes to be used as a 'dope', use of a florescent coat at a spot or two, laser holography and computer based video disc technology of storing data and its quick retrieval. These parameters ofcourse have to be supplemented by other factors depending on the material of the individual art work. It is needless to stress that all these recorded parameters have to be studied and interpreted in a right perspective as a National policy. Such a characterization has to be kept secret so that it does not fall in the hands of people of disrepute who are actively involved in this unlawful act.

Such a study would not only authenticate our new acquisitions but it would also document them to fingerprint them so as to protect and preserve them for all times to come. It would also monitor their health right from their entry into a collection so that the process of their decay could be studied time and again to adopt suitable preventive and curative procedures for their conservation. Such a study would not only deter the art dealers of disrepute to combat effectively their unethical act of deception being followed by at least some of them on one hand and remind the collection incharges of accountability of any lapse on their part so that transparency is maintained.

Such a data would also help us retrieve back our artifacts if stolen in future. Such a physical proof on the objects would also stand as a legal proof in the courts of law if need be. Scholars can also refer to the various collections using internet facilities for such a study all over the country or even abroad whereever such a facility is available. Let us put all our resources together to achieve such a project.

Every important artifact, therefore, wherever it must be documented after systematic scientific study as deailed above. Textual, graphic, photographic (visible & invisible radiations), macrography, radiology, U.V. Fluorescence studies, chemical composition, composition of alteration products and deposits which could help in scientific authentication, associated materials of such as fabrics attached with excavated artefacts, soil contents at least partly should be kept for further references, detection of coatings and secret markings with fluorescence materials and many more could go a long way in helping in the protection and conservation of artifacts. This should be done as quickly as possible in order to secure, document and authenticate our National art treasures so that its loot could be stopped for future generation to enjoy and feel proud of the achievements of our forefathers to give strength to our future generations and to stand with dignity as an Independent Nation. Let us take a pledge once again for this at least now and ensure safety of what is our National Pride thus ushering a new era during the 21st century.

There is, therefore, an urgent need for using computer technology in Museums and other cultural organizations to store and retrieve informations on what they have for exhibitions/shows besides what is being done by way of conservation or condition of cultural relics as it stands today for future correlation and study. All concerned need to cooperate in this endeavour. However, existing personnel need to be trained in computer technology and its application to Cultural Property, we should take help and assistance from computer professionals in achieving such a target in a systematic way. Much actually remains to be done to see it through by way of evolving computer base technology and programming them suitably in this specialized field. Much would depend on persons in authority so that priorities could be worked out to achieve the best out of the advancement in Science and Technology available today.

4.3 COLLECTIVE APPROACH

For example, in the context of western art, a portrait painted entirely by Rubens is more of a Ruben than the one in which he painted the face only and an assistant did the rest while works produced by others under his guidance in his studio would be described as of 'Studio of Rubens'. A damaged painting by Ruben that has been deceptively repainted so as to lead the buyer to believe it all in Ruben's own hand is a fake, eventhough in some areas beneath the repainted portion Ruben's own brushwork is still extant. But a damaged portrait repainted by Ruben in his time should not be called a fake. On the other hand a copy of the painting by Ruben is just a copy but if it is made in order to pass as a Ruben's it is a fake.

However, in the Indian context we know that mostly miniature paintings were produced from Master *Charbas* or Stencils where even the colour scheme might have been decided by the Master Artist and others did the rest to complete it. One finds many versions of our great epics done at different times and places or many copies of the world famous works like that of Padshahnama, Shahnama or that of Jayadeva's great lyrical work Gita Govinda. Should we describe them all copies or otherwise? These are some of the issues in authenticity. On the other hand in case of bronze icons every bronze has been cast from a single mould in the past and later the mould gets destroyed in the process to expose the icon. This cast is later worked, chased and engraved individually. Even the engraving of the eyes and eye balls is done just before the installation of the icon in a temple as per religious rites. No two bronzes, therefore, should tally in their final details. Contrary to this if the icon is cast from a rubber mould, as is done these days, it would be a different situation. The issues in authentication has many dimensions eg. artistic, historic and cultural besides the scientific dimension. The problem of authenticity, in India therefore, differs from the western concept of authenticity and has to be judged accordingly. A question is often raised- if a copy is so fine that it can not be distinguished from the real object, is it not just as good? There are many moral and aesthetic reasons regarding why it is not just as good as an authentic work. The whole approach, therefore, needs reconsideration on the part of all concerned-the Art Historian, Historian, Archaeologist, Museologist and the Conservator. All of them should come to a consensus in this regard. Authentication at the time of acquisition, before and after exhibitions abroad and once in a year to monitor health of objects is very necessary.

In view of the large scale faking of artifacts (Plate 10) in India now many cases of fakes are being offered to museums and have come to light. During the author's tenure as Chief Restorer, National Museum, New Delhi he tried to invite attention of authorities and scholars/experts through some of his publications in the Journal Conservation of Cultural Property in India vol. 18-20 (1985-87), vol. 21 (1988) and vol. 24 (1991) on the subject of faking and imitations. Accordingly a provision was made in the relevant procedure to return the objects which are found fakes within a period of three years of their acquisition and a large number of such artifacts were returned during the period 87-91 with active support from late Dr. L.P. Sihare the then Director General, National Museum, New Delhi.

In the recent past mention can be made of two exhibitions highlighting the menance of faking. One was held in 1988 at the Asia Society Galleries, New York entitled 'The Real, The Fake and The Masterpieces' followed by the British Museum, London (1990) on 'Fake ? The Art of Deception'. These exhibitions have highlighted the problem worldover. Later (1994) Nara Conference on Authenticity was jointly organized by the UNESCO, ICOMOS, ICCROM and the Agency for Cultural Affairs in Japan.

In India, however, we seem to move very slowly. The National Museum Institute in collaboration with the Indira Gandhi National Centre for Arts, New Delhi organized a two day seminar on 'Issues of Authenticity of Antiquities' on 22-23 Nov. 97 in which experts connected with Art purchase from government museums including some leading Conservators also presented their view points. Some art dealers were also invited to present their view point.

The author also presented a paper titled 'Problems of Authenticity of Artifacts - A Need for Collective Approach' special mention was made of some painters (Chitrakars) who are making copies of authentic paintings from important collections of our museums. Works of some of them e.g. Chitrakar Bannu from Rajasthan were discussed since the copies made by them are so perfect that it is not possible to distinguish between a copy and its original with naked eye especially while Art purchase committees are selecting art works on the spot. Examples of many cases were cited. Special mention was made of a copy of Laur Chanda painting which has travelled to U.S.A in which the painter seems to have been inspired by a similar painting of Sultanate period in the collection of the Prince of Wales Museum of western

India, Bombay or two copies were made by the original Painter during Sultanate Period (Plate 11). It was also mentioned that the Jaur Geet Govind manuscript in the collection of the National Museum seems to have been heavily repainted before selling it to the museum and the artist who did it even put his name on the body of the manuscript and the reported connivance of some dealers to discredit the A.P.C. of the National Museum. Can this be classified as 'Fake' ?

The scientific dimension which has remained in the background so far can help in deciding authenticity on the basis of scientific studies producing physical evidence to approve or disapprove the view point of experts on similar lines as Forensic Scientist. Instances could be cited where stylistic, iconographic and scientific evidence could supplement each other or may appear in conflict. The problem posed in authenticity studies, therefore, are often more complex and subtle than simple. An art object may differ from similar objects of known and established authenticity but may not differ from scientific studies point of view because the faker has learned to produce work that could pass the tests of the scientists and hence the divergent views or vice versa. The forger might have corrected technically a fake even though its chemical composition/method of making and stylistic attributes may resemble a genuine or authentic artifact of that period and provenance. Examples of an artificially induced radioactivity of a pottery piece or use of exactly the similar pigments in a miniature or producing artificial patina on a metal object etc. could be some examples which could be cited.

The scientific studies to establish authenticity are based on two main approaches: studying the materials and method of construction to ascertain if these are commensurate with the apparent age of the art object and secondly looking for evidence of age such as the formation of patina. Its composition whether it is systematic or haphazard indicating its genuineness or recent origin as the case may be. Reconstructions and embellishments could be detected. We could also find whether there are any unassociated pieces in it which have been intentionally made to look similar or any coatings have been given to hide the reconstruction. The strides made by science and technology in this direction could help us in the task. Various dating techniques and nondestructive methods of analysis could be used. Simple methods of analysis could be used. Simple methods of examination, density measurements, examination under U.V. fluorescence, I.R. reflectography, X-ray radiography, holography, macrophotography and microphotography in situ can help us to look beyond the scope of the naked eye. X-ray fluorescence, X-ray diffraction, Spark source mass-spectroscopy, Neutron activation analysis, Lead isotope ratio studies and Back scattering studies are some of the other techniques which could be used in the authentication studies besides the carbon-14 dating and thermoluminescence dating techniques, Scientific study or stylistic study alone would be unable to judge whether a piece is authentic or not. To be more effective the scientific investigator has to seek the help of an art historian and a museologist to come to conclusions and rely on their cooperation/interaction to establish the correct position and vice versa. It is of no help to declare an object real or fake without such a collective approach to authenticate artifacts whenever needed. Actually by the use of wide variety of scientific techniques stated above a Scientist, combined with stylistic study, broad knowledge to early technology and vast experience in how materials behave can uncover a wealth of information on correct authentication of artifact under study. There is a great need to understand and appreciate the views of others in related fields of expertise. Nothing on the subject should be decided in haste or isolation by the either side. To understand the complete history of the artifact is of utmost importance.

There should be a clear policy of acquisition of art objects. Objects of ancient origin only should be acquired for museums of ancient art and contemporary artifacts should find a place in an institution dealing in modern art. It is, therefore, high time for us to review our acquisition procedures. It would be most appropriate to complete scientific study and documentation of art objects prior to their acquisition or within a mutually agreed stipulated time frame so that artifacts of doubtful authenticity are checked from entering a collection. A committee of Conservation Scientists could be constituted for this purpose on the similar lines as the Art Purchase Committee to accept or reject an artifact The findings of this scientific committee could assist the bigger Art Purchase Committee to select only authenticated art objects at a later date.

Every object which is offered for acquisition must be examined, analyzed, documented (textual, graphic and photographic), macrophotography, X-ray radiography done and studied by all possible nondestructive means as stated earlier with an open mind. Based on all these studies a database may be prepared on a floppy or optical disc using latest computer technology which could be used for future studies on objects coming subsequently in the collection. This type of documentation could be repeated once in a year for monitoring any replacements or decay of objects for purposes stated earlier.

On the similar lines collections should be documented and the information on these could be stored on an optical disc or a floppy so that various styles and iconographic details could be compared to decide authenticity issues on surer footings and solid database rather than only on memory or theoretical knowledge. Files on individual objects or object with similarities could serve as reference for comparing it with data on newly acquired objects. If such a collective approach on the part of everyone concerned is adopted I am sure we can deter art dealers of disrepute from cheating our museums and we can provide public service to all those who are interested in acquiring authentic artifacts.

In the end I would like to mention that it may be possible to authenticate on the basis of the scientific data thus prepared which could easily be produced in a court of law in the country or abroad to prove legal ownership. Such a study would also be an useful addition to knowledge besides safeguarding this priceless heritage resource for all times to come. All institutions should help and collaborate in this project to make it a success.

4.4 LEGAL ISSUES

The Indian Treasure Trove Act, 1878, the Ancient Monuments Preservation Act, 1964, the Antiquities (Export Control) Act, 1947, the Ancient Monuments and Archaeological sites and Remains Act, 1958 and the Antiquities and Art Treasures Act, 1972 and 'Rules 1973 framed are some of the laws enacted in India on the issue, since more comprehensive definition of Antiquity and Art Treasure were defined. Inspite of all these laws smuggling continued unabated by circumventing the laws, lack of proper documentation of artifacts and antiquities that we possess, absence of fingerprinting technology, faking of artifacts where new artifacts are given antiquarian look or old artifacts/sculptures were superficially painted with modern colours to be removed easily in the country of their destination, urge for acquiring easy money, lack of adequate security of our museums and monuments, urge for acquiring old Indian artifacts by people of other countries etc. etc. are some of the reasons for this illicit trafficking of antiquities out of India. It seems that well organised gangs have come into existence in the past 3-4 decades. Many instances have come into notice where copies/replicas were planted in place of originals, artifacts and antiquities were caught by government agencies since these were being sent abroad as crafts. This is only a tip of the iceberg and we presume that a large number of Indian art has landed abroad in the affluent countries where there are art shops dealing in artifacts openly as their laws do not prohibit such a trade.

To me there are two clear situations

(i) The artifacts taken out of India prior to our independence in 1947 and

(ii) Art objects taken out after independence due to reasons stated above illegal ofcourse.

Our experts had a tough time to retrieve some of these from other countries in the absence of proper scientific records, scientific analysis data and proper fingerprinting to substantiate our legal claims to prove ownership in court of law in those countries abroad. I am glad to report that the Govt Museum, Chennai has completed the fingerprinting of some of their valuable bronze collection with the help of the Deptt. of Science and Technology, Govt of India having provided financial assistance for the purpose to the Indira Gandhi Centre for Atomic Research, Kalpakam, Tamil Nadu. Efforts of Dr. R. Kannan, Commissioner of Archaeology and Museums, Chennai with the assistance of Dr V. Jayraj, Curator, Chemical Conservation and Research Laboratory, Govt Museum, Chennai need to be appreciated in this direction. I only wish that other departments at central and state level would follow suit to protect our art treasures so that they do not land up in the illegal art market in India or abroad.

It is, therefore, high time our government at centre or state should tighten up the measures to safeguard our art treasures from this menance and also improve the implementation of rules/regulations more firmly with all their might without loss of further time.

4.5 SCIENCE IN THE AID OF THE DETECTION OF FAKES

Since the middle of the last century, a new development in taking out illegally the art of India took place. Much of Indian Art had already landed abroad during the past couple of centuries. The art connoisseurs of these countries crave for the possession of Indian antiques in the form of a stone or bronze idol or an oil paining or a rare piece of ivory. Many examples of this have come to limelight in the past decade and I am sure many more are still unknown. This, ofcourse, is a grave problem but connected to it, is another serious problem viz faking and possible replacement from collections besides cheating the genuine art collectors, museum authorities and art connoisseurs by fakes passing as original antiques and art objects. This is the sinister aspect of the illegal act which even experts sometimes are not able to check. Two examples which are very famous for this replacement by fakes are the cases of the famous Shivpuram Nataraja's idol when a replica was planted for the original and the second is the example of the famous Amin Pillars which are reported to have been replaced from the *Malkhana.* There may be many more such cases which might have gone unchecked so far and many may come to surface later. The situation is, therefore, grave and unless checked at the right time may go beyond control.

Detection of fakes is being done on the basis of stylistic considerations but the margin of errors are often considerable. Time and again there are reports of confiscating of antiques by government agencies but in the absence of any scientific authentication, these may go out unnoticed even though these may be museum worthy. The law enforcing agencies do not have cells of antique experts who can quickly distinguish the fakes from the originals and vice versa. Many countries, therefore, consider counterfeiting of an antiquity as an offence and have enacted laws to check this forgery and fake business according to news paper reports coming every now and then. These acts cannot be enforced only by law but need involvement of people at large. It has also been reported that lack of proper museum movement in the country was itself responsible for such an activity as the various concerned agencies did not offer adequate facilities for their conservation or the prices offered for acquisition of these art objects were still very low. However, it is not the case today. Museums do offer good prices for art objects and now some of the art dealers, who are not genuine, are trying to cheat the museum authorities also. They usually offer as one lot some genuine and some fakes to museums with a view that some forgeries may go unnoticed in the process which may make them rich overnight. One such exemplary case was detected in the National Museum which was able to act as per recent policy formulated by its Administration and return the art works not found genuine within three years of their acquisition. Only four out of the twelve Ivory pieces were retained and others were returned being of doubtful authenticity. These were offered to the National Museum in the year 1988 by a dealer who had supplied earlier a few ivories. These were taken by the National Museum on approval basis since there was no unanimity among the members of the A.P.C on their authentication. It was also decided then and there that the help of the Laboratory may be sought to have the scientific view on these ivories.

(A) Scientific Study of Ivory

The scientific study in this direction was based on the following steps.

(a) Iconographic study of the carvings and their relation to similar objects already available in the collection.

(b) Examination of the patination (i) Chemical (ii) Under U.V.

(c) Chemical composition of these pieces

(d) SEM studies to study the composition of the structure and depth of cracking pattern

(e) Study of the cross section i.e. transverse section.

According to iconographic study, all the pieces looked to be as if these were all of the 17th century and the carvings were superb. The details of the carvings were of a very high quality workmanship and artistic excellence. All the minute details of the carvings were so perfect that on stylistic grounds these would pass off as genuine. (Plate 12) These were also well comparable with similar objects in the collections wherever these existed. The collection of the National Museum was scanned for the purpose.

The patination, however, was not similar on these Ivory bedposts and in some cases it looked as if some coating has been given which was coming out with solvents. One of them had a textile piece of modern origin attached to it which could be dislodged with chemicals. Eight of them differed under U.V. lamp from four of the lot. Four of them gave a greenish, yellow fluorescence while the rest of the eight gave the usual blue to purple fluorescence proving that these are not naturally genuinely patinated. It suggested that eight of them were artificially patinated to make them look old by giving them some superficial coat.

(B) Faking of Object of Copper and Its alloys

Copper and its alloys have been used for making artifacts and statues since very early times. The two common alloys namely bronze and brass are remarkably suitable for this purpose because of their excellent casting properties and beautiful appearance of the alloy, either in their original colour or after ageing in a noncorrosive environment i.e. after patination. A newly cast or surface finished bronze has a fine rich golden colour whereas brass has a pale yellow appearance whereas brass would become brownish but with a yellow tinge. In a corrosive atmosphere, these objects may acquire either a greenish or bluish green patina as it is usually called instead of incrustation of harmful type.

The term 'patina' or 'patination' is used rather loosely in connection with the surface appearance of objects of copper or its alloys. It is preferable that the word 'patina' should be restricted to protective type only e.g. the bluish green patina or basic copper sulphate or basic copper carbonate or reddish brown patina of cuprous oxide or blackish patina of cupric oxide which once formed, provides a protective film over the underlying metal so that further corrosion does not occur. In such a case the patina is said to be 'noble' provided it has very little thickness and the underneath artistic details are clearly visible. Incidentally, this is the type of finish some sculptors or authorities consider desirable from aesthetic point of view but there seems to be no unanimity on this subject.

From scientific point of view, as far as this type of patina is concerned, it has only a cumulative effect and as a fine thin layer, it is a proof of its antique value. It is also very hard to reproduce artificially and any attempts to fake such objects can be identified under a sterio-microscope and/or a Scanning Electron Microscope with EDS system by physical and chemical examination of the surface structure. It may not be out of context to mention here, that this type of greenish blue patina, even if it is thick on comparatively modern object, is said to be of aesthetic importance as some of the modern sculptors may desire their objects to have this look. But in case of ancient objects having minute details, we cannot take for granted this theory since it is bound to hide the fine details of the art objects.

It is true that a patina is noncorrosive in nature and we might think that there is a remote possibility that such a natural finish or patina might be the ultimate aim of the creators of the past also. Secondly, most of these statues were for worship, especially in India. Therefore, these were occasionally coated with materials greasy in nature or vermillion. We should realize that there is no justification for the so-called 'overcleaning' of these objects. The attempt has to be to thin down the incrustations to make the minute details clear rather than to remove them completely as has been the case, in the past, in many laboratories. We should not aim at removing every thing from the surface because patination or the accumulation of mineral alternation products is a natural phenomenon.

At times, when an object of such a composition has remained buried in the soil having saline surroundings or when these were kept in an environment near the sea, a corrosive type of incrustation grows on the objects at the cost of the object itself and the object is said to be suffering from 'Bronze disease' which is dangerous for the very survival of the object. In this process, we come across the chlorides of copper either in cuprous form (green) or in the cupric form (Pale grey chalky crust). A question naturally comes whether to remove this type of incrustation or to stabilize, after neutralization of the chloride content. This is a matter of great importance and should not be attempted in haste. Our attempt should be to stabilize rather than risk total removal so that the fine artistic details become clearly visible as far as possible. A well trained conservator knows how far to go and where to stop. We should aim at thinning down these incrustations rather than their total removal.

Besides the above mentioned alteration products when such an alloy object is recovered from the soil, some other corrosion products are also found on the surface of such objects and are of various chemical composition depending on the soil these were buried in. Some of such alteration products are described below:

1. Basic Copper Sulphate (Bluish green)
2. Sulphides (Dark Brown or Black)
3. Nitraters (Bluish green to Blue)
4. Calcareous Deposits (White to Sandy in Colour)
5. Rust deposits (Brownish red)

These would produce an altered affect on the object and as a result, the details may not be clearly seen. In fact it would cover the real beauty of the object. From the foregoing paras it would be clear that these objects may have a varied appearance ranging from white, muddy, pondy brownish, black grey, different grades of blue and green and at times brownish red also.

It is not possible to lay down general rules about how an object of thick deposits should be treated or would look like after treatment, as each case is individual. It should be our aim to arrest the continuing decay so that these objects may continue to provide the beauty of their conception, fitness of their craftsmanship and inspiration associated with their use of enjoyment and at the same time without disturbing the original look of the object as far as possible, by devising a suitable mode of treatment.

The patination or development of incrustation due to pollution is a natural process. The difficulty arises when an object has been patinated artificially and the owner claims it to be an old and genuine piece. Fakers are aware that their skill cannot be judged by simple visual examination unless they leave some clues and make some mistake while doing the faking job. They also try to reproduce the common patinas on these objects by methods better known to them.

An artist friend of mine gave the following information about patina on bronze/brass images as is usually done on the sculptures in order to get different shades of the patina.

1. For greenish shade

    Copper Nitrate : 50 gm

    Sulphuric/Nitric Acid : 75 cc

    Water : 300 cc

2. For light brown to black shade :

   Liquid Ammonia : 200 cc

   Barium Sulphate : 25 gms.

3. For Reddish Brown :

   Ferrous Sulphate : 25 Gms

   Sulphuric Acid : 200 cc

4. For Brown :

   Potassium Bicarbonate : 25 gms

   Liquid Ammonia : 200 cc

5. For antique effect :

   Acetic Acid/Vinegar

   Imly water/Lemon water

   Electroplating process

The antique type patina may be produced artificially but the extent of erosion cannot be produced perfectly. The old corrosion is usually deep seated, layered and is hard to reproduce. Immediately on the metal surface is the green patchy cuprous chloride layer, followed by an oxide layer on the whole surface and all other layers, if present would be on the top of this uniform oxide layer if the patina is genuine. It may not be possible to reproduce this genuine uniform patina of smooth and shining oxide layer which comes with the natural oxidation process and is hard to produce by artificial means like heating with a blow lamp. What we find on such objects may be a sulphide film which has a colour resemblance with the oxide layer (brownish black) or copper oxide mixed with organic resin solutions coated on the objects. Basic copper carbonate layer of permanent nature is hard to produce and what is produced easily is either copper acetate or copper sulphate or copper nitrate by using the respective acids or their acidic salts or copper carbonate mixed with resin solutions and coated on the object. At times, wax polish mixed with the required colour is also used. Attempts have also been made by some fakers to reproduce even the 'Bronze disease' by either pouring hydrochloric acid at a few spots or by keeping the whole object in hydrochloric acid fumes or other acid fumes. Such objects after artificial patination look dry and are usually given a wax polish to get glossy finish so that they may look genuine and old. In other words, these objects are made to look as antiques while they are not. Incidentally, no genuine patina should be soluble in organic chemicals which would prove its recent origin. Some Copper hoard objects (Plate 13) having induced patina were reported to be fake a decade back as these could not stand various tests.

It is a hard fact that so far we have no direct dating method for metallic object on scientific lines such as carbon-14 or Thermoluminescence dating for organic and clay objects. Presently attempts are being made at various research centres to find out a theory for dating metallic objects on the basis of composition especially of the trace elements and impurities in them. But very little can be expected from them as they do not have collections of their own and museums may not be in a position to supply them samples readily unless these research centres are affiliated to them.

Extreme care is, therefore, necessary while acquiring such metallic objects for museums or private collections if we are interested in the old and genuine artifacts which, I am, sure, we are.

Today, forgeries exist in large numbers in the art market, in private collections and in museum collections. Most forgeries can be identified by a combination of inconsistencies in style and iconography, in method of manufacture in metal and corrosion structure and in the elemental composition. However, there are many exceptions to these generalities to exclude the use of elemental composition alone as a test for authenticity. The important evidence of its authenticity is metallurgical :

1. Metallographic examination of a cross section
2. Microscopic study of the surface of the object
3. Natural and long term corrosion
4. Method of fabrication should be of the relevant period
5. Thermoluminescence dating of the core material if any before radiography.

The other side of the picture is the one where genuine temple statues bronze or brass, are finding their way into some rich private collection, a curio shop in the country or abroad. The Hindustan Times, July 6, 1986, reported in very strong terms, in its editorial entitled "Sinning against Man and God" about vandals robbing our ancient temples of invaluable works of art. The works of art ultimately are bought up for fabulous sums by those who have no dearth of money and who may hold their priceless possessions a secret atleast for a decade or so.

The editorial further states, "Even when the vandals are apprehended, they get away either scot free or with an incredibly light punishment". These persons who are deeply engaged in such a nefarious trade have been flourishing at the cost of several thousand temples specially in Tamil Nadu, Andhra Pradesh, Kerala and Karnataka. These temples, it is needless to say, are either ill guarded or are not guarded at all which is very favorable for such an activity. All efforts to safeguard against such a menance have been found ineffective.

(C) Faking of Miniatures

Faking of art objects has increased in the last few decades in India, eventhough elsewhere it has been going on for a number of decades now. There were famous forgeries like the 'Piltdown' forgery detected in 1953 which rocked the art and archaeological world. Since then, many instances have come to light and are well known all over the world and India is no exception.

The problem, therefore, is very serious. We should realize why this is happening. Spurt in this activity may be attributed to the following factors:

(a) Art market is gradually becoming empty of genuine ancient art objects.

(b) Countries of origin prohibit old art objects from going abroad and, therefore, art dealers of disrepute often break the laws of the country.

(c) Due to mass tourism, fakes travel as genuine art objects and vice versa.

(d) Prices have gone up exorbitantly and disproportionate to their prices twenty years back, thus making the business very rewarding which would make the fakers rich overnight.

(e) With material progress, people, in general, are becoming more and more art conscious thus increase their demand which may be exploited.

Faking of metal and wooden ethnological objects came to notice earlier also. During recent studies, we came across the faking and forgeries in respect of paintings, ivories and even stone objects. This has become a major problem for museums today, besides keeping their holdings in a good state of preservation for posterity. Scientific study takes longer time for which the objects have to be subjected to detailed technical study. The scope of this study is confined to what is the preliminary examination of some characteristics with a trained eye or using a low magnification hand lens can contribute checking the problem to some extent. To study only the iconographic or stylistic attributes is not enough. One has to go a little deeper to be on the right track. The faker is bound to make some mistake.

As per information gathered from various sources, the following artists are reported to be engaged in the revival of ancient art of miniatures :

Pahari Miniatures –	Master Sansar Chand, Retired Curator of Dogra Art Gallery, Jammu, who has learnt art of making miniatures from Shri Jagar Ram Chunni.
Rajput Painting –	Sangram Kala Sangrah is engaged in this since 1981 and the following artists are working there. He has trained about 50 artists so far. Jaisingh Govindji Jagdishji Mahendra Singh
Jaipur School Mughul/Tibetan, Pahari, Persian & Rajasthan	Ved Pal Sharma alias Bannu of Jaipur
Western Indian and Rajasthani paintings	Badri Lal *Chitrakar* of Bhilwara and his five sons
Paintings on ivory	Ghori of Jaipur

Besides these, various Art Schools have copying of miniatures in their syllabus and therefore, there would be many artists engaged in this work in different parts of the country.

Attempt at these ateliers is to adhere as closely as possible to the materials and methods used in the traditional miniature paintings. The artists base the works on the scores of paintings of various schools which are made available to them and they have access even to several incomplete studies which form part of the collections. At Sangram *Kala Sangrah*, Jaipur, the artists are given a painting to work on. The composition is first traced meticulously from the original on to extremely fine handmade paper which is fashioned at Sanganer, when placed by the side of the originals the copies lack nothing in richness and vivacity. Shri Ved Pal Sharma of Jaipur also known as Bannu is another artist whose services are sought after by masses and connoisseurs for restoration of damaged paintings. Asked how a layman can distinguish between his modern pieces and the works of his ancestors and their contemporaries, Bannu replied 'you cannot'. But Bannu finds nothing wrong in that, as Indian Art, unlike Western Art, is a reflection of the glory of the art itself and not of the Artist.

It is reported that the faker photocopy original works on paper and treat them chemically so that they acquire an antique colour and sell them as originals, thus, a leisurely shopper may find more than one original of the same painting in the market at one time. Many times persons connected with this trade officially visit museums and libraries in the garb of scholars and see the original miniatures in the collections and get them photographed in colour for their future use, scholarly or otherwise. With the introduction of a colour copier the work has become much easier. In many cases, they hunt for partially damaged miniatures or even drawings which could be repainted or even painted as the case may be and later use some surface coating which would alter their look into old. They use old pigments, grind them as per earlier tradition and use paper which is already old and at times damaged.

The National Museum Laboratory had purchased a few decades back some copies of miniatures from open market. Out of these, three miniatures were studied on the basis of their style in consultation with the then Dy. Keeper (Paintings). The point under study was whether in the collection, we have original miniatures similar to those copies with us. Except in one case, the remaining two had no equivalents in the collection but may be in other collections elsewhere. One was very similar to an original in the collection (Front & back cover). These were subjected to further detailed study. However, in the two other cases also it was not possible to distinguish the original and the copy with naked eye. This has, therefore, made a more detailed study necessary to come to conclusions on sound footings.

(D) Exploitation of Artists

One very important aspect of the problem is the exploitation of the innocent craftsmen to reproduce metal replicas of the original images. As a matter of fact, size to size copies should be banned to deter faking or possible replacement. Sales of 'antiques' in luxury hotels or in museum art shops thorough out the country is common. Most of these, however, may be clever copies where new objects are made to look old.

Such an activity has been going on for the past 4-5 decades now. The most talked about example is that of the Sivapuram Natraja which has recently been returned to the owners having being smuggled out of the country a few years ago. This image is 4 feet tall and weights 100 kg and according to a report, was purchased by Nortan Simon Foundation, U.S.A for a fabulous price of 1 million dollars after changing many hands since it left India. From the size and weight of this image it could be seen that if an image of this size could go out of the country, then small size statues would be easy targets. The famous Sivapuram Nataraja was one of the five images found at Sivapuram in 1951. The local authorities decided to install this image in a newly built temple and accordingly gave it for cleaning. The cleanig job having been entrusted to a Sthapathi, the original was smuggled out of the country in 1956 or so but not before its cast was made. The copy was later installed in the newly built temple at Sivapuram. Apparently, this Nataraja image was cleaned by the Sthapathi and later it was also sent to London by the U.S. Foundation for cleaning in 1964. The Indian Government filed a suit in 1976 and it was decided that the image would be returned to India in 1986.

The Sthapathi was not a Conservator or Restorer but a Sculptor wanting to get rich quickly; it is possible that he was mere interested in its copy being made for replacing it rather than in its cleaning. This so-called 'operation cleaning' by unscientific means to me looks to be the root cause in promoting replacements or the possible smuggling of these temple possession out of the country. During my visit to the states of Karnataka, Tamil Nadu, Kerala and Andhra Pradesh I found statues of bronze being over-cleaned i.e. completely stripped of their old patina. Everyone can imagine that the visual appearance of such an over-cleaned image could neither be differentiated from the cast of the same image nor from the photographs (B/W) of the two, thus the customs can easily be fooled by the exporters in such a case. As a matter of principle, therefore, no one should ever try to overclean the old images in order to deter their replacement now or in times to come. It is always safe to keep them a little undercleaned.

(E) Scientific detection of fakes

(a) X-ray analysis

Artificial patina (Bronze disease) – Oxychloride

Natural patina (Bronze disease) – Basic copper chloride

(b) Differential Thermal Analysis

New oil paint – Inadequate polymerization to have distinctive and characteristic thermal reading.

Old oil paint – Complete polymerization which takes about 100 years and thus differs from above.

(c) Mass spectroscopy

New metal object (lead) – Lead 210 concentration higher

Old metal object (lead) – Lead 210 concentration nil (half life being 50 yrs only)

(d) Fluorescence study

New marble – Red violet flurorescene

Old marble – Spotty bluish yellow fluorescence

New ivory – Blue to purple fluorescene

Old ivory – Greenish yellow fluorescence

(e) Radiology

New crackle – Does not show in X-ray

Old crackle – Shows in X-ray

(f) XRD studies

Struck coins – Diffraction Pattern is constant

Cast Coins – Diffraction pattern is irregular

(g) Thermoluminescences studies

Old object – Considerable natural thermoluminescences

New object – Very little natural thermoluminescences.

(h) Use of some pigments whose date of manufacture, invention are known could guide in dating them e.g. Purssian blue (1704), Artificial ultramarines (1820), Emerald green (1814), Zinc white (18th cent), Cobalt blue (19th cent),

(i) XRF studies could help in comparing artifacts with each other during the centuries i.e. large number of artifacts are subjected to this study and an atlas could be made of these findings so that a change could be detected.

(j) Macrophotography through a Stereomicroscope to record surface features such as brush work, foundry marks, small and minute defects, signatures etc.

(k) Radiology for recording internal features/defects such as additions and alterations and depth of cracks. Method of fabrication.

(l) Precision Photography for recording dimensions, measurements and intricate details.

(m) Laser Holography for 3D characterization.

(n) In-Situ Metallography for microstructural characterization and defects.

(o) Neutron Activation Analysis for detection of trace elements.

CHAPTER V

Ethics in Conservation

5.1 PROFESSIONAL ETHICS

Examination of ethical problems in the field of conservation are not new and some of the related problems have been debated in the past in various forums the world over. In India also it is high time to take stock of the situation and discuss these issues at this juncture for taking timely steps. However, one wonders why we are taking about ethics in conservation and on a second thought the answer comes to mind suggesting that there are some unethical things which are going on in the profession. International Council of Museums, Paris (1987) published a Code of Professional Ethics which was adopted unanimously by the 15th general assembly of ICOM meeting in Buenos Aires, Argentina on 4th November 1986. It provides a general statement of professional ethics, respect for which is regarded as a minimum requirement to practise as a member of the Museum profession. The aspect has been dealt with in greater detail by them.

One of the essential ethical obligations of the present day museum professionals is to ensure that the collections are passed on to future generations in as good and safe a condition as practicable. This is possible only with the collaborative efforts of all concerned, whether a Director, Curator, Scientist, Conservator or Restorer by ensuring adequate conservation technology for preventive and curative conservation including the provision of suitable environmental protection against the known natural or artificial causes of deterioration of art objects and museum specimens. There are, therefore, professional ethical responsibilities of all concerned in this joint venture which binds us very firmly to pass on the heritage to our future generations intact because it is this past heritage which transmits to us the bulk of the knowledge of our past.

(A) Conservator/Restorer

Specialists with diverse expertise work with the objects of art but the material survival of the art work itself is subject to the knowledge, discipline, sensibility and intelligence of the Conservator/Restorer who works physically on them. He is the one who enjoys the most intimate contact with the object on which he works and thus with those who made them. The procedure which he/she adopts include examination, documentation, consolidation and cleaning. In this process he gathers intimate and hitherto hidden or less visible messages, an object has in it which help in discovery of information about the past and better understanding of man's cultural heritage. With the modern day advance in science and technology, a Scientist can throw light on many aspects of the objects, which was not possible a few decades back. A Conservator-Restorer is, therefore, more equipped today to conserve an object but we should not forget here that he/she may also ruin it by destroying and altering the hidden information which were not readable with out use of X-ray, UV and infra red rays before actual intervention and inappropriate treatment may alter chemical and physical structure in the crystalline configuration of the constituent material or matter which in its original state would allow scientific study leading to correct information about its period, provenance and method of fabrication even though it might have deteriorated to some extent. Minimum intervention which is absolutely inescapable, would therefore, be the best policy to follow. Moreover, the skill with which a Conservator-Restorer would undertake, restoration treatment is going to matter most if it is decided to undertake treatment on an object. His/her work, therefore, assumes great responsibility towards heritage of man. A critical analytical approach should always succeed rather than attitudes which have their roots elsewhere. Conservation profession should not be allowed to be misused to lead to suppression or falsification or distortion of evidence for the sake of economic, political or other purposes for wrong aesthetic considerations or out of pure humananity. This is the worst enemy of the conservation to a point of no return. Hence responsibilities are loaded with professional ethics.

(B) Ethics in Conservation

The ethical issues which highlight the basic purposes and requirements can, therefore, be summarized as under :

1. Who should be authorized to undertake conservation/restoration?
2. What should be the degree of replacement or restoration of lost/damaged parts ethically acceptable to art historians and others in the profession?
3. What should be the nature and extent of the remedial action to retard or prevent deterioration of or damage to the cultural property?
4. What is the need of complete physical and chemical examination/documentation of the state of the art work before and after restoration?

5. Why there is a need to have a collaborative approach, before deciding a scheme of restoration with fellow workers, Curators, Scientists and Art Historians?

6. Why the detection of fake and forgeries is becoming complicated day by day?

7. Whether Conservators/ Restorers are professionally or status wise comparable with Art Historians, Museologists or Archaeologists or Scientists?

(C) Policy on Replacement or Restoration

There are often difficult decisions to be made in relation to this aspect regarding the lost parts of an object. The one most important is that the new additions by way of restoration should be ethically acceptable to all including the art historians and the decisions to replace should be in joint consultation rather than unilateral by one or the other acting alone. The fundamental approach here is that a Conservator/Restorer does not create a new cultural object. They only ensure that the object should be able to stand the vagaries of the environmental conditions, problems of display, handling, packing and transport efficiently as its aesthetics in order that the object secures physical strength to stand its own weight or norms of its aesthetics/ artistic prerequisites. Normally, therefore, what can not be preserved or what does not exist physically or what needs physical strength for its safety need to be restored. In other words extent and nature of restoration has to be decided first alongwith the choice of new materials to be added. Modern materials are preferred because they are more readily distinguished and could be removed if necessary. He/she should also know how far to go and when to stop. Obviously, there are limitations and restoration has a special position in conservation which has to be carried out with utmost care. This involved expertise of a surgeon comprising of manual art and skill. Linkages have to be established with manual skill, theoretical knowledge and capacity simultaneously to assess a situation and to act upon it atonce keeping the overall impact of these together. Different policies are being adhered/followed by different workers in this respect. In the Indian context most of the institutions are following the policy in which added portions may be easily distinguished but at the same time they do not deter the attention of the viewer and the art work may be appreciated aesthetically. A balanced view is always in the forefront and is preferred. In case of an oil painting, however, the added arts are kept a little under tone leaving scope for future changes in tonal values.

5.2 REMEDIAL ACTION TO RETARD THE PACE OF DECAY

All matters undergo change since deterioration is a law of nature. Conservation is an attempt to retard this process of decay by controlling the physical, chemical and biological factors interacting with materials. It is in fact a race against the time (Plate 14). The chemicals used should be conducive to the originals and should not have any deleterious effect on it. They should not change the chemical structure and its aesthetics. It should be absolute minimum and reversible in view of the constraints. If these principles are followed by Conservators there would be scope to improve by future workers according to the advancement of science and technology in times to come or change in thinking of the whole aspect in future. Unfortunately some institutions/ museums in India still use the old time practice of using the objects and when these are damaged, simply hide them in their stores to be lost for posterity. Conservator should resist such acts on the part of Curators and instead convince them that such objects may be restored. Such a dialogue and collaborative approach on the part of Restorers and Curators would go a long way to preserve art works in their collections.

Faithful visual and microscopic examination of the present physical state of an object, as it is today, is essential in order to distinguish between the original and added parts, if any. It is a factual position in the life of the object whether or not it has undergone deterioration and to record the nature and extent of human intervention it has experienced since it was made. We have to distinguish between the intervention that enhances the qualities of the object and that which is detrimental to its integrity. Each object contains-singly or combined-historical stylistic, iconographic, technological, intellectual, aesthetic and/or spiritual messages and date. It is, therefore, essential that any treatment is preceeded with a complete documentation, visual, microscopical, graphic, photographic or employing techniques which make use of U.V., IR and Xrays. This would help to achieve the complete synthesis of the problems interpreting the results and imparting restoration accordingly.

Help is also taken of the simultaneous study made by the Art Historian, Chemist, Microbiologist, Geologist, Metallurgist to have an assessment of the problems connected with the particular object on long term basis including the course of treatment one propose to follow. This ofcourse is the ideal situation and needs patience on the part of all concerned including the Curators and Museum Directors. Complete record of all new materials added to the object should be kept to help noticing any change in the object, interpreting results quickly and foreseeing the consequences.

The need for collaboration between experts of various but connected disciplines assumes great significance for proper execution of restoration to an object. They must understand the view points of each other, their concepts, approaches and their responsibilities. Together they should decide all ethical issues connected with the profession or to the general public. Such collaboration/ consultation would deter all controversies which might arise after the restoration process is over. The Conservator/Restorer should have scientific and logical arguments to support and prove all actions so that these could be communicated to other fellow workers and also to the Curators who hold collections at the various stages of restoration process. This would take care of many problems which might arise due to lack of proper communication.

(A) Misuse of Scientific and Conservation Techniques

In Europe for centuries, reproducing masterpieces was an accepted and widely practised method of student artists for polishing their techniques. Indian artists also followed this practice during British Raj. Copying later fell into disrepute in mid-1880s with the rise of status conscious elite and emergence of the Art Dealer. Lately a large number of instances have come to light where scientific knowledge about artifacts has been exploited by forgers and fakers. A possible collusion of people who know the art objects and methods of their restoration, have raised doubts for such an unethical crime. Such attempts become detectable at high magnifications and may escape the eye. Scientific tools can confirm the detection of such fakes and forgeries under expert examination and correct interpretation of results.

John Dornberg in his paper 'Artists who fake fine art have met their match in the Laboratory' is an eye opener. Professional ethics, therefore, need to be observed strictly by all concerned. Exploitation of Archaeologists, Museologists, Curators, Modelers, Artists, Restoration personnel and Scientists has to be checked through professional restrictions and mass public condemnations of these culprits.

5.3 STATUS OF CONSERVATORS/RESTORERS

The author in his paper 'State of Conservation in India today-Conservation needs better treatment' tried to focus attention on this but situations do not change so quickly. O.P. Agrawal in his recent comment 'the Conservation Conundrum' has attempted to pinpoint public attention as to why optimum utilization of available resources is not being done in a meaningful manner. He says when planning of management of cultural property is done it is very seldom that a conservation expert is consulted or his advice sought. In the process quite often field of expertise such as art history, archaeology, paintings, anthropology, decorative arts etc. and therefore, it is reflected in their thinking as well as actual implementation. Conservation/restoration gets low priority and is thus considered a routine matter and is looked after by a person of lesser status. This gives rise frustration and is not conducive to the actual needs. Why acquire or why excavate if conservation is not given a due place. It is better for art objects to remain buried or with the art collectors rather than spending huge public money on them to deteriorate in a museum. There is, therefore, a great need for a trained Conservator/Restorer in a museum, provide him/her with adequate funds to build up infrastructure and also give due status at par with others if not higher. He/she should also be involved with art acquisitions or excavations as the case may be. Setting up of a training institute in the National Museum, New Delhi for art history, conservation and museology has raised our hopes for brighter future for conservation profession in general and museum conservation in particular.

The cultural heritage of India is so rich and varied in its range and content that it represents the personality of India as a Nation. Our climatic conditions and other forces of destructions, natural or man-made, are constantly at war with this pride of ours. In theory, though it should be in practice also, therefore, the need and importance of conservation of this heritage cannot be overemphasized, not merely because of its role in National development, but because of its academic importance. It follows as a corollary that conservation should get adequate importance in the various institutions charged with responsibility of preserving (Plate 15) our cultural past.

Today, the authorities are thinking to prepare inventory of cultural properties of national importance because of the overpublicized damages that our rare art works are reported to have suffered due to their frequent travel abroad, mainly because of their unmanageable sizes or because of their physical condition. There can be no two opinions that rare and unique objects of art should not be sent out of the country. From the point of view of the physical condition, unmanageable size and fragility of some art objects, their frequent travel abroad should also be discontinued to save them from any further possibility of damage. There is need to have an expert committee which should look into this aspect of the problem. Its verdict should be binding on the organizers.

Even after so many years of our independence, the conservation facilities in the country, in terms of men and money, still remain disproportionate (Plate 16) to the quantity and quality of the heritage, no matter whether it is archaeology or museums or archives or libraries. Budget for conservation is only a fringe of their total budget and the conservation facilities at our command are not encouraging. We sometimes forget that it is the conservation of the holdings of an institution which keeps the institutions alive and if art objects decay the institutions cannot exist anymore.Conservation profession in general and conservation scientists in particular, therefore, need better treatment so that they could discharge the responsibility with their full heart and vigour.

During the past three to four decades, many conservation laboratories have been set up but they still remain under the minimum need level. In many of them, only a few hands are available, with inadequate facilities at their disposal. These hands have received training at the various institutions of the country but still remain incapable to handle the objects independently. Most of these trained persons have left conservation as a profession and have taken up other lucrative jobs because they know that many people in their profession even having international recognition could not get better treatment as regards getting higher posts during their tenure in their respective departments. The Conservation Scientist or Restorer continues to get third rate importance in the heirachy of institutions. The Restorers continue to work behind the scene and tolerate with patience. The patience and tolerance they have to use in the treatment of art objects is being used by them for tolerating indifferent treatment towards them. It is anybody's guess as to who would suffer as a consequence.

5.4 CONCLUSIONS

The Chemistry Branch of the Archaeological Survey of India, with its headquarters at Dehradun, the Regional Laboratories at Hyderabad, Dhar and Bhubaneswar or Zonal Laboratories at Delhi, Chandigarh, Vadodra, Agra, Aurangabad, Ajanta, Mysore, Jaipur, Madras and Patna continue to serve in the monumental task of saving our monuments by practical conservation.

The National Research Laboratory at Lucknow has a beautiful building of its own now and is well equipped as regards staff and equipment to do useful research work which is helping other institutions of the country. It has opened a regional Laboratory at Mysore to look after the needs of the sourthern part of the country. However, facilities for actual conservation need to be augmented manifolds even in this laboratory.

The Conservation Laboratory of the National Museum continues to contribute its share to conservation of antiquities. It is helping the NMI in its two year Degree course in Art Conservation to freshers and is conducting a three month training course for in-service personnel of the country. It is also helping institutions of neighboring countries. National Museum Institute (A deemed University) of Art History, Conservation and Museology have produced ten batches of Conservators/Restorers since 1989.

The laboratories of the National Archives continue to serve the cause of conservation of archival materials of the country. They have centres at Bhopal and Pondicherry which are doing good work taking into consideration the facilities at their command. The States Archives are also doing their part.

There are other laboratories which are contributing to meet the challenge of conservation, namely the laboratories of the Indian Museum, Calcutta, the Salarjang Museum, Hyderabad, the Government Museum, Madras, the Baroda Museum and Picture Gallery, Vadodara, the Directorate of Archaeology and Museums, Rajasthan, Jaipur, the Regional Conservation Laboratory of Archaeology, Trivandrum, Department of Archaeology and Museum, Patiala, the Govt. Museum & Art Gallery, Chandigarh, the Bharat Kala Bhavan, Varanasi, the National Library, Calcutta and the Victoria Memorial Hall, Calcutta. All other laboratories have a single man outfit. Such laboratories are not many and they continue to work in isolation.

Studies in Archaeological Chemistry made by late Prof. K.M.T. Hegde of M.S.University, Baroda and Dr. H.C. Bhardwaj of the Banaras Hindu University of Varanasi need a special mention. Both of them have done commendable work in their respective fields.

The needs of conservation as per the latest situation are therefore, as follows:

1. There is a need to provide adequate budget for various laboratories in the country. Every museum should have a conservation unit.

2. Present training programmes should be strengthened further.

3. Research in conservation techniques and technical studies of art objects should be organised more systematically.

4. Problem of fakes and forgeries in art objects should be studied in detail for proper authentication to help museums in acquiring objects.

5. Studies on proper dating and characterization of art objects should be carried out.

6. The senior Conservation Scientists with long experience should be given appropriate status in the various setups of the country.

There is a great need for a National Conservation policy to take care of the connected problems as one unified authority which could be heard by all. There should be no rivalry among such helping hands since our's is a vast country and there is so much to do for every one. With economic opening up, collaborations could be arranged with institutions of repute from abroad on equal partners basis by institutions having expertise with them in the country. The time is, therefore, ripe and fit for appraisal by all concerned, pooling our resources together in terms of expertise, involving public to create awareness about conservation, seeking help from people who have it, creating more and more facilities for conservation at the governmental or private levels and gradually bringing all artifacts under care of experts to save them from forces of decay. The challenge before us, therefore, is not one but are many. What is most needed is the whole hearted effort to save our heritage for future generation to see and cherish. Let us not allow the challenges to overpower us and face them with all our skill, knowledge, expertise and above all the will to do for the cultural wealth of the country. Let us take a pledge once again to save the artifacts from destruction or atleast retard the pace of deterioration after 55 years of our independence with renewed efforts by all concerned.

There is an urgent need for integrated environmental approach so that in the name of development people living in various countries do not contribute in the degradation of the ecology of the past. Our approach should be strictly environmental friendly by enforcing the regulations and ethics of clean environment. Development is necessary for developing countries to make more and more people economically sound but it has to be sustainable based on nature conservation. The recent fire in a plastic Garbage market-Jwala Puri in West Delhi many others in several cities in India remind us of the urgency so as to save materials worth crores of rupees but also ensure safety of the residents of the nearby colonies from hazards of such an accident. Naturally such places have to be far away from the residential areas.

Governmental concern at the 1992 Rio Earth Summit emphasized the need for sustainable, environmental friendly, global ecology. Only Government efforts cannot achieve these goals without the support of public at large. Voluntary organizations could assist in organizing and planning programmes on the importance of friendly ecology. Efforts in this direction, therefore, have to be concentrated at various levels and should be taken up with all the seriousness to save the ecology and heritage for generations to follow us. Let all of us pool our resources and knowledge together in this monumental effort to the best of our ability and contribute our bit in this direction to save the mother earth from a possible global disaster. An equilibrium has to be established between human needs and the ecology around us. Let us learn to live with nature rather than abuse it. As regards monuments like Taj are concerned we should not take chances in the light of the conflicting view points expressed by various experts between 1976 and 1995 on the one hand and the government, on the basis of the ASI reports, on the other.

As regards fakes and forgeries, in this category of objects attempts are going on to cheat museums in particular and art collectors in general. For museums and art collectors from abroad, the attempt is to produce artificial aging on comparatively new objects and for smuggling out of the country old objects are repainted with modern paints to look as new in order to cheat the

Archaeological Survey in India. It is needless to say that such objects later on landing in a foreign country would be carefully cleaned to reveal their original look. There are a large number of art dealers and souvenir shops in every city of the country where such attempts are in practice. Museums have to take the problem very seriously so that only genuine art objects are acquired for their collections.

In the National Museum, New Delhi we have devised a procedure under which art dealers will have to return the money paid to them if during three years of the acquisition of a particular object is discovered later that the object is of doubtful authenticity and such an object would be returned to the seller. In this context it would be recalled that large museums abroad undertake full technical examination of an object if it is to be procured for the museum prior to its acquisition. A systematic study to eliminate fakes and forgeries may be undertaken by the National Museum in order to solve this problem. This ofcourse is a time consuming process and a work of great patience.

Further it could also be decided as a matter of policy that objects of metal are not overcleaned and a small portion of the art object restored is left untouched to compare it with their deterioration in future so as to save the evidence as a part of history of Arts as well as History of Science. Such objects can never be duplicated with a view of faking as it would not be possible to create different corrosions or alterations on the same object and art works should not be judged by eye only but by scientific means by experts in the line i.e. Art Historians and Art Conservators with an open mind devoid of any preoccupations/prenotions.

It is, therefore, of utmost importance that adequate measures are taken intime so that the genuineness of the collections could be ensured and the unethical act of faker and forger could be stopped in the interest of the Art and Culture of this great country for all times to come with collaborative efforts of Art Historians, Art Conservators and the Administrators at the government as well as at the non-governmental professional levels. Museums, therefore, should get their collections authenticated as per scientific studies which have developed in the recent past quite significantly.

The problem is very great and unless something is done right now, it might become more complicated. The question now is what to do, so that museums and genuine art collectors are not cheated. One more thing comes to mind and that is whether results of technical study of art objects be kept in files only or these should be published. We have to keep in view that fakers might take advantage of these results to fabricate their forgeries which would circumvent the scientific study. The Conservation Scientists have to be ahead of the forgers. Museums should not acquire art works in haste. They should consider all the pros and cons and continue to involve experts of right type in acquisition of art objects for their respective collections.

Museums, art lovers and art connoisseurs have to exercise great care while acquiring works of art for their collections. All sorts of attempts are being made by fakers to cheat the art lovers exploiting their artistic and aesthetic urge for such objects in the country and abroad. Art acquisition should be done with utmost professional expertise and ethics. In one case objects worth seven lakhs of rupees were returned to the dealer, when I was Head of the Conservation Laboratory of the National Museum, New Delhi.

The future study, which can be undertaken should be on the following general outlines;

(a) Identification of artist materials from paintings whose authenticity, provenance and period is known so that comparison could be made.

(b) Photography, macrophotography, IR reflectography and radiography.

(c) Study of patina and ageing of the painting.

(d) Earliest manufacture dates of some pigments are known and therefore, their presence to be checked.

In conclusion it would be said that museum collections should be made more educative for which the display has to be appropriately modified so that it is more communicative and conservation oriented. More stress is to be laid on understanding the symptoms and mechanism of decay so that preventive measures could be adopted accordingly as per the needs. The concept of a Curator-Conservator, collective approach to conservation, total care and safety of objects has to be adopted. Once the collection is acquired, periodic monitoring of their condition and monitoring of environmental parameters of decay are some of the steps which could help to a great extent in preventing further decay of such objects. Incharges of collection should not make the problems of conservation more complicated in any way. They should know what to do and what not to do. The repairs has to compatible, tested and long lasting rather than quick and one time effort which could do more harm than good in the longrun. There should be an interaction with various specialists and a conservation policy has to be chalked for a particular collection. Collective responsibility and accountability are the need of the hour to ensure adequate measures for protection, care, preservation and display of artifacts. These are some measures of management which the museums of National importance or otherwise are expected to ensure for them and render help on the similar lines to smaller museums in their region. We can thus take measure for the conservation and protection of the collections which would go a longway to ensure safety of the cultural relics of the past for future generation to see and feel proud of. Let us meet the challenges with our concentrated efforts in the direction. All branches of Museology, Archives and Archaeology should have conservation oriented approach. Display, excavation, storage, handling and transportation etc. has to be accordingly systematic as per standards of cultural management.

Bibliography

Rao, T. Shivaji, "Environments and its Effect : Threat to Taj and its Environs", *Conservation of Cultural Property in India, Vol. XII* (1979), 13-16.

Prasad, Lallan Kumar, "Pollution and its Effect on Marble Monuments". *Conservation of Cultural Property in India, Vol. XIII* (1980), 19-25.

Agarwal, O.P., "Conservation of Taj Mahal - The Real Problem", *Conservation, Preservation & Restoration Traditions, Trends and Techniques, Proceedings of the International Colloquium organized by the Birla Archaeological and Cultural Research Institute, Hyderabad,* January 1995, 1-14.

Bisht, A.S., "Prevention and Eradication of Biodeterioration in Museums - A study of Problems and Future Prospects", *Report presented at the VII Indo-US Workshop on Conservation held at Washington,* May 1987.

Bisht, A.S., "Control of Biodeterioration in Museums–A study of Problems", *Biodeterioration of Cultural Property, Proceedings of the International Conference held at NRLC,* February 20-25, 1989, Lucknow, 98-103.

Shaheen, Fauzia and Dhawan, Shashi, "Natural Plant Products : A safe Preventive Measure Against Anthrenus Vorax (Coleoptera: Dermestidal)", *Biodeterioration of Cultural Property, Proceeding of the International Conference held at NRLC,* February 20-25, 1989, Lucknow, 186-194.

Thomson, Garry, *"The Museum Environment",* Butterworths & Co. Ltd., 1978, Chapters on Air Pollution, 124-154 and 228-249.

Shiva, Vandana and Holla Bhar, Radha "Intellectual Piracy and the Neem Tree", *The Ecologist,* Vol. 23, No. 6, Nov. - Dec. 1993, 223-227.

Thomas, Christopher, "Pollution eats into India's Marble Glory", *a report The Times,* Saturday, February 1, 1992.

Raver, Anne, "From the Ancient Neem Tree, a New Insecticide" *a report in the New York Times,* Sunday, June 5, 1994, 49.

Aldhous, Peter, "Neem Chemical: The Pieces Fall in Place", *a report in Science, Vol. 258,* 6 November 1992, 893.

Sharma, Devinder, "The West's Waste - Plastic Basket", *a report in Hindustan Times,* Thursday Nov. 17, 1994.

Dogra, Bharat, "Caution: Health Hazards Ahead", *a report in Hindustan Times,* Wednesday, Nov. 16, 1994.

Ghosh, Nirmal, "Let's have No Free rides for Offenders", *a report in Hindustan Times,* Monday Nov. 21. 1994.

Datta, Pankaj Kumar, "Use of Neem Oil in Conservation", *Conservation of Cultural Property in India, Vol. XVIII-XX* (1985-87), 98-100.

Shah, A.R., "Application of Cashew Nut Oil as Wood Preservative", *Conservation of Cultural Property in India, Vol. XXIII* (1990), 28-29.

Devi, Dhanpati L., "Experiment on The Application of Artemisia Oil as Insecticide and Insect repellant in The Museum", *Conservation of Cultural Property in India, Vol. XXII* (1989), 108-111.

Prasad, Lalan Kumar, "Role of Neem Leaves in Protecting Textile Materials and Paper Documents", *Conservation of Cultural Property in India, Vol. XIV-XV* (1981-82), 95-97.

Tandon, B.N. and Singh, S.P., "Chemical Cleaning of Marble Surface of Taj Mahal Using Absorption Clay Pack Method", *Conservation of Cultural Property in India, Vol. XVI-XVII* (1983-84), 87-89.

Singh, S.P., "Some Problems on the surface of the Taj Mahal", *Conservation of Cultural Property in India, Vol. XXII* (1989), 91-95.

Hot Chand, "Environmental Assessment of a Thermal Power Station in Rajasthan", *Conservation of Cultural Property in India,* (1992), 3-5.

Kharbade, B.V. and Agarwal, K.C., "Scientific Elucidations of Peacock Feathers Believed To Be Used As A Preservative For The Manuscripts', *Conservation of Cultural Property in India,* (1992). 99-108.

Prakash, Anand O., "Neem as a Medicinal Plant", *Science Reporter, Vol. VIII* (No. 2) Feb. 1976.

Mathur, M.S., "Monuments in Marble - Some Aspects of Their Degradation", *Conservation of Cultural Property in India, Vol. IX* (1976), 48-56.

Report of the Expert Committee on Environmental Impact of Mathura Refinery, 1977, 27-30.

Toishi, Kenzo, "Radiography of the Great Buddha at Kamakura" *Studies in Conservation, Vol. 10,* No. 2 (May 1965), 47-52.

Stambolov, T., "The Synergism of Ammonia and Sulphur dioxide in the erosion of Monuments by Acid Rain", *ICOM Committee for Conservation, 9th Triennial Meeting, Dresden, German Democratic Republic,* 26-31 August 1990, Preprints Vol. 1, 366-372.

Lal, B.B., "Weathering and Preservation of Stone Monuments", *Conservation of Cultural Property in India, Vol. II* (1967), 1-36.

Bisht, A.S., "Patina on copper objects and its alloys", *Conservation of Cultural Property in India,* Vol. XVIII-XX (1985-87), 5-10.

Bisht, A.S., "Technical Study of Seven Phophner Metal Images", *Journal of Indian Museums,* Vol XXXXII (1986),71-84.

Bisht, A.S., "Macrophotography for basic Characterization of Miniature Paintings, *Journal of Indian Museums,* Vol. XLV,(1990), 18-20.

Bisht, A.S., "Authentication of Art objects at the time of acquisition or return from abroad - a problem", *Conservation of Cultural Property in India,* Silver Jubilee volume (1991), 3-7.

Bisht, A.S., "Authentication of Artifacts : Conservator's point of view", *Studies in Museology,* M.S. University, Baroda, Vol. XXX.(1997), 21-25.

Chandra Sekharan P., "The Pathur Nataraja case at Royal Court, London", *Paper presented at Astech-97 (21-25' Oct' 97) at Kalpakam organised by INGCAR & Govt. Museum, Chennai sponsored by DST, Govt. of India* (1997).

Jeyaraj, V., Rao, C. Babu, Venkataraman, B. Jaya Kumar, T. and Raj, Baldev, "Authenticity in Art Bronze Icons", *Proceedings of the National seminar on aspects of protection, presentation, care and display of art objects in the Museums of National importance held at Salarjung Museum, Hyderabad 18th & 19th Aug' 97* (1997).

Raj, Baldev, Rao C. Babu and Bhattacharya, D.K., "Fingerprinting of South Indian Bronze Idols", *Current Science,* Vol. 62, No. 6, 25 March (1992).

Venkatraman, B., Rao, C. Babu, Bhatacharya, D.K. and Raj, Baldev, "Radiography of Medieval Investment - Cast Idols of India", *British Journal of NDT,* Vol. 35, No. 10, Oct. 93.

Harinarayana, N. "A system of recording chemical conservation work" *Studies in Museology,* Vol. 1(1965), 40-41.

O.P. Agarwal (Ed.) "Documentation in Museums" *Proceedings of the 1973 All India Museums Conference held at Mysore,* Sept. 19-23, 1973, Museum Association of India, New Delhi.

Kuhn, H. Zocher, C., "Feature cards for the storing of Technical Data which result from the scientific examination of works of Art", *Studies in Conservation,* Vol. 15, No. 2 (May, 70), 102-121.

Oddy, W.A., Barker, H., "A feature card information - Retrieval system for the general museum laboratory" *Studies in conservation,* Vol. 16, No. 3 (Aug. 71), 89-94.

Rensbergr, John, M. and Berry, B. William B.N., "An automated system for Retrieval of Museum Data" *Curator,* Vol. X, No. 4 (1967), 297-317.

Light, R.B., Robers, D.A. and Stewart J.D. (Eds.) "Museum Documentation System, Developments and Application", Book-Butterworths, London, 1986.

Kirsten Grimstad (Ed.) *Proceedings of the 8th Triennial Meeting, ICOM Committee for Conservation*, Sydney (1987) Vol. 1.

Devkar, V.L., "Applied Technology in Museums", *Journal of Indian Museums,* (Feb. 1991), New Delhi, 132-13.

Penniman, T.K. "Pictures of Ivory and Other Animal Teeth, Bone and Antler". Book, Pitt Rivers Museum, Oxford (1952)

Savage, G., "Forgeries, fakes and reproductions : a handbook for the Art Dealer and Collector", Praeger, New York (1964).

Amau, F. "The art of the Faker : Three thousand years of deception" Book Translated from the German by. J. M. Brownjohn, Little Brown, Boston (1961).

Williamson Muller, G.C., "The book of Ivory", London (1938).

Maskell, A.O., "Ivory in Commerce and in the Arts", *Journal of the Royal Society of Arts* (1906), Vol. 54.

Radlcy, J.A. and Grant, J., "Fluorescence analysis in Ultraviolet light", Book, Chaymen and Hall London (1959).

Dwivedi, V.P. "Indian Ivories" Agam Kala Prakashan, Delhi (1976).

"The Week" (August 14-20, 1988), 62.

"Miniature Painting : In search of Excellence" Swagat, January 88. 46-50.

"The Week" (March 20-26, 1988), 32-33.

"The Week" (March 13-19, 1988), 32-33.

Andhare, D. Shridhar, "Chronology of Mewar Paintings" Agam Kala Prakashan, Delhi (1987).

Leledov, L.A "Professional Ethics in Restoration" *ICOM Committee for Conservation, 8th Triennial meeting Sydney* (6-11 Sept. 87) Preprints Vol. II, 545-548.

Jedrzejwska, H., "Ethics in Conservation" Booklet, Stockholm (1976).

Code of Professional Ethics, Booklet ICOM Paris (1987), 24-25.

Ward, Philip, "The nature of Conservation- A race against Time" Book, the Getty Conservation Institute, California.

The Conservator-Restorer : A Definition of the Profession, ICOM News, Vol. 39. No 1 (1986), 5-6.

He deals in fake masterpieces, Hindustan Times, Nov 7, 1987.

Bisht, A.S. "Science in the Aid of Detection of Fakes with Special reference to Ivories : A case study" *Conservation of cultural property in India,* Vol XXII (1989), 31-35.

Domberg, John, "Artist who fake fine art have met their Match in the Laboratory" Smithsonian (Oct 1985), 60-69.

Bisht, A.S. "State of Conservation in India today- Conservation needs better treatment." *Four Decades of Conservation in India–Problems and prospects NRLC, Lucknow. Proceedings of a Seminar* (June 29-30, 1988), 39-40.

Agrawal, O.P. "Comment- The Conservation Conudrum" *the India Magazine of her people and Culture,* January 1989, 38-39.

Torraca, Giorgio, "Relation of Relative Humility to wall Paintings preserved under ground level", *Conservation of Cultural property in India* (Edited Bisht, A.S., Bhatnagar, I.K. and Singh, S.P), Agam Kala Prakashan, Ashok Vihar, Delhi (2000), 138-1140.

Ginell, William, S. "Making it Quake Proof" *Museum News* (American Association of Museums) 69, No. 3, 61-63 (May-June 1990).

Van Buskirk and James E. "Disaster in SanFrancisco" AAL and News Letter, The News Letter of the Association of Architectural Libraries, 9, No 1. 3-5 (June 90).

Corno, Elisabeth and Bone, Lesley, "Seismic disaster Planning; Preventive Measures make a difference" News Letter (Western Association for Art Conservation) 13, No 3, 13-19 (Sept 1991).

Agbabian, Mihran, Ginell, S., William S, Masri, Samu F. and Nigbor, Robert L. "Evaluation of earthquake damage mitigation methods for museum objects" *Studies in Conservation,* 36, Nos. 111-120 (May 1991).

Feilden, Bernard, "Between two earthquakes : the management of Cultural Property in Seismic zones" *In proceedings, Old Cultures in New Worlds : 8th Geneva Assembly and International Symposium ICOMOS 1987,* 582-589.

Chutkow, Paul, "Preparation for a showdown on the fault line" The New York Times, (Dec 2, 1990) 441, 443.

Musson, Melvyn; and Crook, Humprey, L., "Earthquake Preparedness Planning", *Disaster Recovery Jounrnal,* 4 Nos (Jul-Sep 991) 30-33.

McGavin, H.L., "Earth quake protection of Essential Building Equipment" Book, John Willy and SMS, Newyork (1981).

"Reducing the risks of nonstructural earthquake damage; Practical guide", BAREPP 85-10, Bay Area Regional Earthquake Preparedness Project, Oakland, California (1985).

"Data Processing facilities : guidelines for earthquake hazard mitigation " VSP Association, Sacramento, California (1987).

Mathews, M.S., "Rehabilitation and Retrofit of Earthquake Damaged Monuments in Gujarat" Abstracts of *the International Seminar on Conservation of Stone Objects with Special reference to Limestone Objects,* 18th to 21st Dec 2001, Government Museum, Chennai, 23-25.

Barclay G. Jones, "Protecting History Architecture and Museum Collection from Natural disaster," Book, Butterworth publishers, 80 Montrale Avenue, Stoncham, MA 02180 (1986).

Podany, J., "Advances in the reassembly of large stone sculptures at the J. Paul Getty Museum" in *Recent Advances in the Conservation and Aanalysis of Artifacts, Institute of Archeology, London* (1987), 375-381.

Isliyama, Y., "Motions of rigid bodies and criteria for overturning by earthquake excitations" *Eearthquake Engineering and Structural Dynamics 10* (1982), 635-650.

Meriam, J.L., "Statics" Book, John Wiley and Sons, New york (1986).

ICOM Statutes–*Code of Professional Ethics,* ICOM Maison de 1 UNESCO, 1 rue Miollis, 75732 Paris (1987).

Keish, Bernard, "Secrets of the Past-Nuclear Energy Application" in Art and Archaeology' U.S. Atomic Energy Commission (1972).

William J. Young (Ed.) Application of Science to the Dating of works of Art, *Proceedings of the Seminar Sept 23-25, 1974, conducted by the Research Laboratory Museum of Fine Arts Boston,* Massachusetts, U.S.A.

"The Real, The Fake and the Masterpiece", *Catalogue of the Asia Society Galleries- Exhibition organised by them* from June 11- August 28, 1988

Mark Jones (Ed.) "Fake? The Art of Deception" *Catalogue published by the British Museum of the Exhibition organised by them* in 1990.

Strong, Rod (Jr.), "Security of works of Art Functional Photography" (March/April 86), 6-17.

Dawson J.E. and Gupta K.K., "Authenticating Bronzes - Myth or Reality' *C.B.I Bulletin,* Vol. IX No. ii, Nov 2001, 20-27.

Singh, S.P., "Role of Plants in the Environmental Protection of Monuments", *Conservation of Cultural Property in India* Vol. XXIX (1996), 179-189.

Singh, S.P., Nagta, P.K. and Gupta, K.K., "Radiographic Documentations in the National Museum, New Delhi" *Conservation of Cultural Property in India,* Vol. XXIX (1996), 222-230.

Jeyaraj, V., "Characterisation of Bronze ICONS in the Govt. Museum, Chennai", *Conservation of Cultural Property in India,* Vol. XXX (1997), 182-191.

Rodriguez, Placid, "Radiography of Ancient South Indian Panchaloha Idols" *Conservation of Cultural Property in India,* Vol. XXXI (1998), 4-16.

Sharma, B.R.N., Mangiraj, V.R. and Trambake, R.S., "Scientific Documentation in Conservation of Monuments" *Conservation of Cultural Property in India,* Vol. XXXI (1998), 141-147.

Raj, Baldev; Rao, C. Babu and Bhattacharya, D.K., "Fingerprinting of South Indian Bronze Idols", *ASTECH - 1997,* Vol. 2, 445-450.

Bhatnagar, I.K., "Some Thoughts on Fakes and Forgeries", *ASTECH - 1997,* Vol. 1, 271-274.

Senapati, S.K., "Computerisation of the documentation activities in Conservation Laboratories : a Challenging task", *Conservation of Cultural Property in India,* Vol XXV (1992), 93-96.

Gupta, K.K., "Problems in Authentication of Paintings" *Conservation of cultural Property in India,* Vol XXVI (1993), 60-65.

Saini, S.S. and Verma, I.B., "Environment Management at Mathura Refinery" *Conservation of Cultural Property in India,* Vol XXVII (1994), 12-25.

"Science and Technology in the Service of Conservation ", *Preprints of the IIC Washington Congress 982,* Published by I.I.C., London.

Index

D

E

G

H

Q

R

S

Illustrations

Plate 1

Plate 2

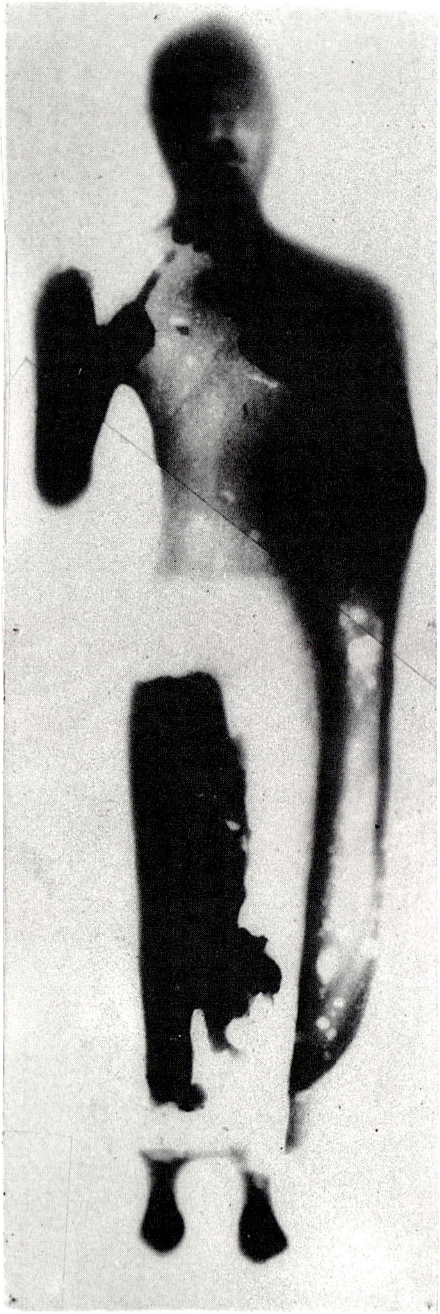

Plate 3

Plate 4

Plate 5

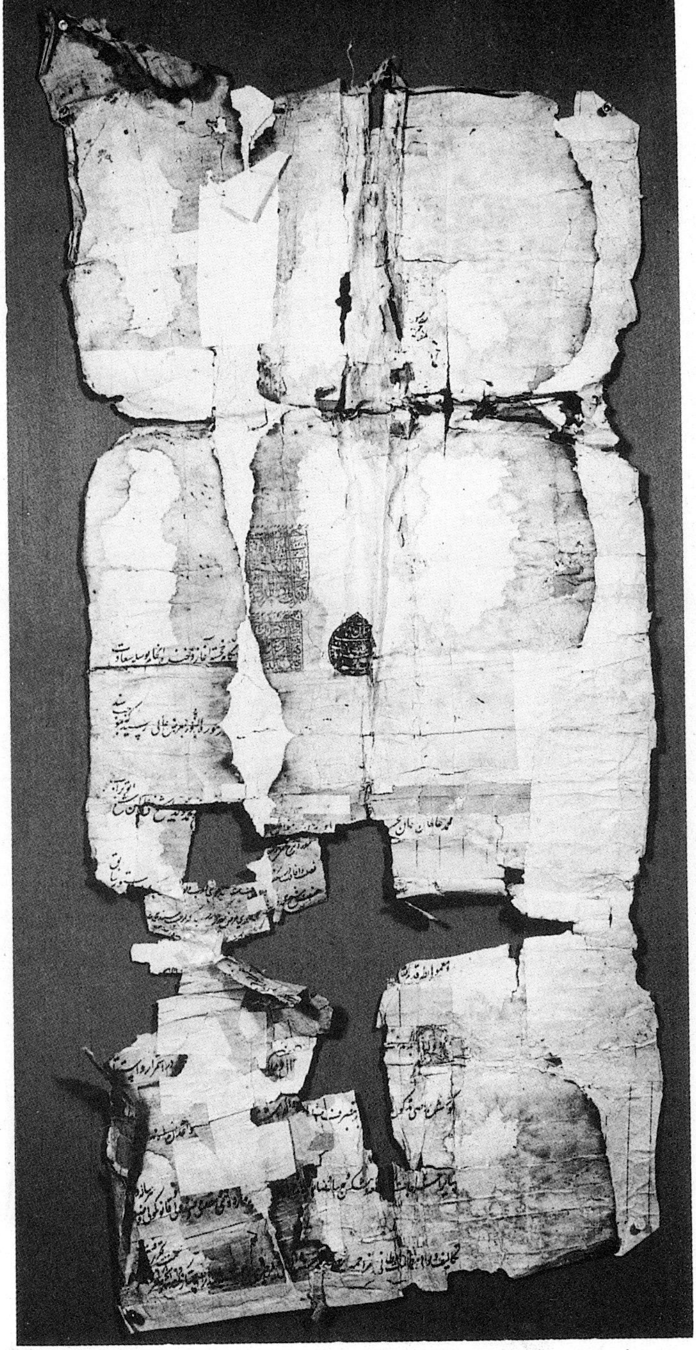

Plate 8

Plate 9

Plate 10

Plate 11

Plate 12

Plate 13

Plate 14

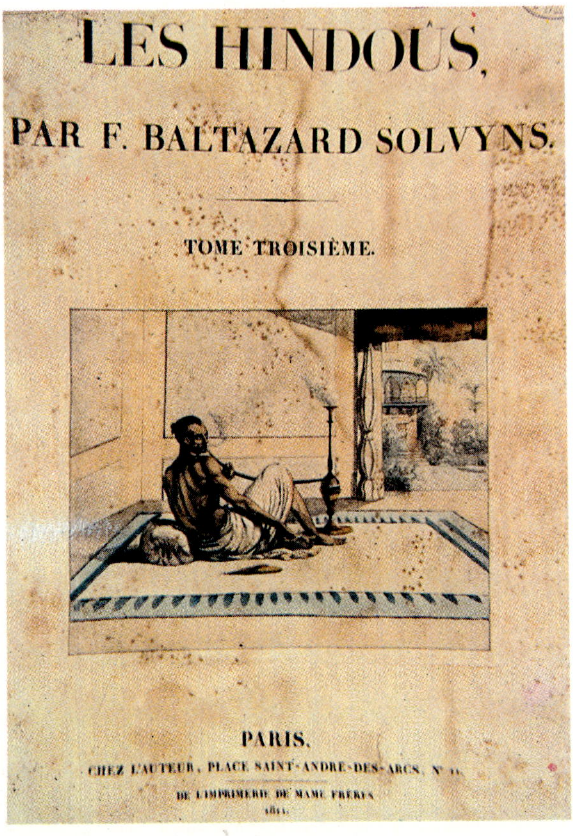

LES HINDOÛS,

PAR F. BALTAZARD SOLVYNS.

TOME TROISIÈME.

PARIS,

CHEZ L'AUTEUR, PLACE SAINT-ANDRÉ-DES-ARCS, N° [illegible]

DE L'IMPRIMERIE DE MAME FRÈRES

[illegible]

Plate 15

Plate 36

Nanostructured Materials Preparation via Condensation Ways